Preaching and the
Thirty-Second Commercial

Preaching and the Thirty-Second Commercial

Lessons from Advertising for the Pulpit

O. WESLEY ALLEN, JR.

AND

CARRIE LA FERLE

WESTMINSTER
JOHN KNOX PRESS
LOUISVILLE · KENTUCKY

First edition
Published by Westminster John Knox Press
Louisville, Kentucky

21 22 23 24 25 26 27 28 29 30—10 9 8 7 6 5 4 3 2 1

Book design by Drew Stevens
Cover design by Mark Abrams

Library of Congress Cataloging-in-Publication Data

Names: Allen, O. Wesley, Jr., 1965- author. | La Ferle, Carrie, author.
Title: Preaching and the thirty-second commercial : lessons from
  advertising for the pulpit / O. Wesley Allen Jr. and Carrie La Ferle.
Description: First edition. | Louisville, Kentucky : Westminster John Knox
  Press, 2021. | Summary: "Believing that preaching can benefit from
  advertising's laser focus on how to make its message stick, O. Wesley
  Allen, Jr. (a preaching professor) and Carrie La Ferle (a professor of
  advertising) have written this first-of-its-kind book on what preachers
  can learn from advertising"-- Provided by publisher.
Identifiers: LCCN 2021011145 (print) | LCCN 2021011146 (ebook) | ISBN
  9780664265441 (paperback) | ISBN 9781646980772 (ebook)
Subjects: LCSH: Preaching. | Advertising.
Classification: LCC BV4211.3 .A4255 2021 (print) | LCC BV4211.3 (ebook) |
  DDC 251--dc23
LC record available at https://lccn.loc.gov/2021011145
LC ebook record available at https://lccn.loc.gov/2021011146

Most Westminster John Knox Press books are available at special quantity discounts when purchased in bulk by corporations, organizations, and special-interest groups. For more information, please email SpecialSales@wjkbooks.com.

Contents

Preface to the
"Preaching and . . ." Series

Preachers are not just preachers. When they step into the pulpit they are also theologians, storytellers, biblical teachers, pastors, historians, psychologists, entertainers, prophets, anthropologists, leaders, political scientists, popular culture commentators, ethicists, philosophers, scientists, and so much more. It is not that they are expected to be masters of homiletics and jack of all other trades. Instead it is that when preachers strive to bring God's good news to bear on the whole of human existence, a lot is required to connect the two in existentially appropriate and meaningful ways.

The Perkins Center for Preaching Excellence (PCPE),[1] directed by Alyce M. McKenzie, has worked with Westminster John Knox Press to create a book series that contributes to that work in a new way. While homiletical scholarship has long drawn on the full range of biblical and theological disciplines as well as a variety of philosophical and rhetorical disciplines, this series attempts to push the interdisciplinary dialogue in new ways. For each volume, the PCPE brings together as coauthors two scholars—a homiletician and an expert from another, nontheological field to bring that field into conversation with homiletics in a way that offers both new insights into preaching as a task and vocation and new strategies for the practical elements of sermon preparation and delivery.

This volume brings together the first two "odd bedfellows" of the series, as the authors refer to homiletics and the study of advertising. Preaching and marketing/advertising serve significantly different purposes, but the sermon and the ad share a same central concern: how to get a message heard in today's noisy and changing communication environment so that it might have its intended impact on its intended audience.

O. Wesley Allen, Jr.
Series Editor

1

The Problem

The question driving this book is what can preachers, who shape sermons (monological speeches that last anywhere from twelve to forty-five minutes), learn from the best of advertisers (who must communicate their message in thirty seconds or less). Granted, preaching and advertising are odd bedfellows. In one sense their purposes can even seem to be opposed. Whereas advertising celebrates culture and promotes the values of commercialism and materialism, the gospel proclaimed in Christian pulpits is often critical of and countercultural to and promotes values that challenge a materialistic worldview. Moreover, advertising and preaching employ radically different media.

In another sense, however, the purposes of preaching and advertising are aligned: both are communicative endeavors aimed at persuading the audience to consider new options for their lives. As such, they both also share some similar hurdles to jump over in order to present those new options effectively, hurdles not present for advertisers and preachers of the past.

MULTIMEDIA NOISE

It has been two decades since the twenty-first century began, and in that time the world has changed dramatically. According to *Business Insider* (2018), the global population went from 5.9 billion in 1998 to 7.6 billion in 2018, while 2007 found the world's urban population surpassing that of people living in rural settings.[1] Technology has allowed more people to communicate around the world than ever. Social media did not exist in 1998, but today more than two-thirds of Americans are on Facebook, with more than 3 billion worldwide estimated to be using social media by 2021. According to the Pew Research Center, in 2019, 81 percent of Americans owned a smartphone and 96 percent owned some type of cell phone device.[2]

In today's multimedia world, people are barraged with communication all day, every day. It is not just the information age but the age of constantly competing information. In such a setting, both preachers and advertisers struggle with how to get people to hear a unique and specific message, engage it, and respond to it, instead of that message simply being lost in the noise or ignored in the midst of stimulus overload. According to the CEO of Hootsuite,[3] the average consumer in the United States in the 1970s was exposed to five hundred ads per day. Today many estimate that number has jumped to five thousand per day. For advertisers the new question becomes, how do you get consumers to notice and take interest in a product or service in the midst of a plethora of competitors all striving for attention? How, for instance, is a single thirty-second commercial to stick with consumers when television, radio, websites, billboards, and social media venues present them with thousands of advertisements every day? Similarly, how is a twelve- to forty-five-minute sermon on Sunday to stick with hearers when it must compete with seven days of the people being barraged by and attending to different values being promoted by advertisers, politicians, news pundits, television, movies, magazines, Twitter feeds, friends at work, and Facebook friends from the time they rise in the morning until they go to sleep at night?

POSTMODERNISM

In addition to the significant increase in the amount of information available to consumers and congregations, multimedia technology has also helped create a situation in which no one person or institution is an authority or expert and everyone is able to contribute to and distribute online content. The shift from one-way communication based on a centralized broadcasting source to a decentralized, social media and individually driven environment has not only broken down traditional parameters of time and space but also has redefined communities, individual identities, and communication norms.

This is part of a shift from a modern to a postmodern epistemology that has been under way since the middle of the twentieth century. In the modern era, truth was viewed as absolute. What is true in New York is true in Wichita, Moscow, and Cairo. Persons and institutions with the correct knowledge, then, were authorities who could declare what was true in specific arenas. In the young, postmodern era, however, truth is viewed as local, relative to perception. "That may be true for you, but this is true for me." People *choose* what is true for them. In a sense, what has happened is that meaning has replaced truth as the category by which people align their lives, even though they continue to use the word "truth" to describe what they consider meaningful. Indeed, whereas in the past people sought to discover "truth" to be applied to all, today they "make" meaning for themselves and are fine with others doing the same.

One result of this shift is that, in our postmodern culture, authority has shifted from reason to experience. People are less persuaded by truthful facts than they are by meaningful experiences. What does this mean for advertising? With an emphasis on multiple realities and continually fragmented presents, people do not buy products for their functional use as conveyed by an advertiser via linear transmission.[4] People buy the lifestyles that products represent to help them create and experience multiple identities to enhance the meaning of their life stories.[5] Consumers want to co-create meaning, reinvent themselves continuously, and use products and other symbols to represent different life projects and self-identities. Consumers want to be included in the process of defining brands, and technology has allowed them to create their own messages and share their opinions en masse at the push of a button.

Preachers have an analogous problem. With the shift from public reason as the authority for discovering truth to individual experience as the authority for making meaning has come a shift from affiliation with and dedication to communal religious institutions to greater emphasis on individualized spirituality. More and more citizens of postmodernity feel no need for a religious authority to speak truth or meaning to them. Just because someone does show up for worship, however, does not mean they are there to listen in the same way past hearers did. They will not simply accept the preacher, Scripture, or the church as having the authority to prescribe meaning for them. They will take from sermons what they find meaningful and discard what they do not.

How can preachers persuade postmodern people to accept the theological message of their sermons when individualized experience has replaced public reason as the authority for meaning-making? Even if preachers are able to be heard through the noise, what new methods might they use to offer listeners experiences of their message, making sure people's hearts are engaged along with the heads?

PLURALISM

The proliferation of forms of communication and shift of authority from public truth to individualized experience is complicated further by the fact that these two dynamics foster and are fostered by a rising pluralism in American culture. Whether true or not, past communicators assumed a shared knowledge base, ethos, and broad value system in our culture. These were, of course, defined by those in power. The "melting pot" was reductionistic, taking the diversity of our population and creating one common stew whose recipe was determined primarily by white, heterosexual, cisgender, Christian men. However, the intersecting civil rights movement, multiple waves of feminism, sexual revolution, rise in immigration from non-Christian countries, and globalization have replaced the "common" with "particulars." Instead of a shared culture we have numerous overlapping yet dividing subcultures. At times we as a culture celebrate such diversity, and at others the pluralism leads to intense conflict. Effective communication is difficult in such a context.

Advertisers not only must deal with the problem of trying to develop long-term relationships with consumers while consumers have multiple brands vying for their attention (multimedia noise). They not only have to deal with the ease with which consumers change brands because their identities are in flux (postmodern emphasis on experience). Advertisers must also adjust their campaigns to the reality that no longer does one size of advertisement fit all. An advertisement that appeals to white, middle-aged men may turn away young persons of color or elderly women. A diverse market makes for opportunities to sell to more groups and individuals, but how does an advertiser reach very different segments of the market?

Preachers also struggle with pluralism. To imagine homogeneity in a congregation is naïve. A preacher may look out over the pulpit and see the pews filled with people who are of the same race or ethnicity, live in the same geographical area, and fit within a certain socioeconomic range. Yet as surely as people in the pews watch different news networks, get their news from late-night talk shows, or watch no news at all, there are differences in values and perspectives in the congregation. Laity are influenced by, participate in, and contribute to a wide range of subcultures that preachers must consider. How does a preacher create a meaningful sermonic experience that cuts through the communication noise of the world and is effective for the twenty-eight-year-old lesbian accountant in the choir, the seventy-seven-year-old man who has ushered every Sunday since he retired from his postal route twelve years ago, the middle-aged couple who bring their children to church only once or twice a month because of their work and their children's sports busyness, and the visitor about whom nothing is known beyond first impressions?

While preachers often lack the tools and resources, advertisers spend considerable time and money to systematically study consumers and communication challenges in an effort to develop effective messaging. Advertisers use a variety of research techniques stemming from secondary research to surveys and interviews to focus groups. Research focused on understanding market segmentation issues such as the needs, wants, values, and attitudes of consumers is very important. Advertisers are also interested in testing different advertising concepts and messages for how they hold consumers' attention, how well consumers comprehend the message, and to what degree they like the ad. Brand recognition and recall are also important, as well as perceptions of brands, satisfaction with brands, and loyalty to brands. Since advertising and preaching share some of the same obstacles in communicating their messages, can preaching benefit from advertising's study, resources, and methods in trying to communicate the gospel more effectively?

HOMILETICS AND ADVERTISING AS ODD CONVERSATION PARTNERS

The initial answer to the above question might seem to be a resounding no. Homiletics and advertising are different disciplines with very different objectives, even objectives in direct conflict. Many people have argued that advertising encourages materialism, leads to poor social values, supports selfishness, and causes insecurities and anxiety.[6] In contrast, the gospel is good, true, and meaningful with the intent to better people and society, to offer them God's grace and justice. Advertisers are primarily motivated by profit. Their goal is to sell products to make money for the stakeholders and to continue to improve profits each year. Conversely, preachers are motivated to liberate people, proclaiming the Word of God, forming people in Christian identity, and offering people Christ. Some advertisers even knowingly provide deceptive messages in hopes of misleading or confusing the consumer in order to garner sales. Such tactics are eventually condemned by the Federal Trade Commission (FTC) and often caught by competitors or consumers, but the practices occur nonetheless. They usually cause short-term damage, such as monetary loss to consumers and market share to competing companies. When conveying the Word to a congregation, preachers work to provide truth as presented in the gospel, helping people find God-given meaning in their individual lives and in the wider world.

The views of advertising listed earlier portray the worst of the field. Indeed, we could easily list the sins of the pulpit in such a way that would show why so many people dismiss the efficacy of preaching. While much advertising may convey radically different messages than Christian preaching, the best of advertising offers preachers approaches and techniques that can be helpful in their communication. For a moment then, let us consider what the best of advertising can look like.

We need to begin by properly defining *advertising*. Advertising in one form or another has been around for centuries, dating back to evidence of ads in the form of posters and notices in Egyptian steel carvings, wall or stone paintings, and papyri. As changes have occurred in economic systems—especially the evolution of free-market capitalism—and with advancements in technology and media—so too has advertising changed. The first U.S. newspaper advertisement ran in 1704 in the *Boston News-Letter* informing readers of property for sale in Long Island.[7] Over the years advertising has grown to become an integral part of our economy and culture. Typically, advertising is seen positively from an economic perspective yet criticized for its social and cultural influences.

A traditional definition of *advertising* is "a paid, mediated form of communication from an identifiable source, designed to persuade the receiver to take some action, now or in the future."[8] However, this definition has been questioned with changes in technology and in light of how brands have had to add value to their offerings by thinking in terms of social responsibility in their business practices and supporting socially good causes and messages. One standard advertising textbook offers a definition that takes account of advertising as not only providing messages about goods and services but also conveying ideas more broadly. The authors define *advertising* as "a paid form of persuasive communication that uses mass and interactive media to reach broad audiences so as to connect an identified sponsor with buyers (a target audience), provide information about products (good, services, and ideas), and interpret the product features in terms of the customer's needs and wants."[9]

Two other advertising scholars, Dahlen and Rosengren, shorten the definition while broadening the scope of coverage to "brand-initiated communication intent on impacting people" and leave open how "impacting" might be interpreted.[10] Traditionally, advertisers have hoped, and often still hope, that impact to be one of persuading an audience to buy the product or service. Today, however, consumers demand that advertisers be held accountable for their products and the culture that advertising messages create. This shift has taken place as the general public has become more aware of and concerned about issues such as threats to the environment and sustainability as well as the ability of consumers to voice concerns about products and related issues online anytime. Strategically, advertisers cannot afford to succeed at any cost today, and in order for brands to flourish they must respect the consumers they serve. This mode of doing business is very different from the announcement and linear style of advertising of the past.

With this understanding of advertising in hand, we can appreciate some of the more positive aspects of the field. For example, in discussing the morality of advertising, one scholar argues that poetry and art are similar to advertising as both try to entice thoughts, produce an emotion, and assert a truth—and each requires an audience for validation.[11]

Advertising can also offer positive images of humanity. An ad for Thai Life Insurance begins with music but no words while viewers watch a young man walking down the street. Runoff water from a spout on the side of a building surprises him when it splashes on the top of his head, but instead of getting upset, he moves a pot with a dead plant into the spot where the water hits the sidewalk. From there we watch the young man do a series of thankless good deeds. He helps an ornery woman get her food cart up over a curb, gives a street dog half his lunch, puts two of the three bills in his wallet in the cup held by a girl and woman begging with a sign that says, "For education," and leaves bananas on the door of an elderly neighbor. All the while observers are watching and shaking their head at the naiveté of the young man. The round of good deeds concludes with the narration, "What does he get in return for doing this every day?"

Then we see the young man doing the same deeds again. The plant is still dead. The woman and child are still poor. Observers still scoff. As we see the young man at home in a small, simple, even poor apartment, the narration starts again: "He gets nothing. He won't be richer. Won't appear on TV. Still anonymous. And not a bit more famous." Then the cycle of good deeds begins again. Only this time the woman with the food cart is laughing and the dog follows him on his way to become his companion. When the man reaches the place where he gives money to the woman and her daughter, the girl is not to be found. The woman is there begging alone, raising a question in the viewers' mind (and that of the young man) about her well-being. But then from behind him a girl's voice yells, "Mom," and the young man turns to see her dressed in a school uniform. The narration begins again: "What he does receive are emotions. He witnesses happiness. Reaches a deeper understanding. Feels the love. Receives what money can't buy. A world made more beautiful." And as the camera shows a small green plant being watered by the runoff water from the spout with a butterfly alighting on one of its flowers, the narration asks, "And in your life? What is it that you desire most?" Of course, the Thai Life Insurance company can help protect people and secure their dreams. But in the end, the advertisement presents the brand in a responsible way with a socially responsible theme focused outside of materialism and financial wealth.

Many other brands also convey positive social messages in the process of promoting a product. In a 2011 advertisement for its smartphone, an LG Electronics ad showed three young adults walking by a warehouse in an urban setting. They see inside an older man by himself working with difficulty to restore an antique carousel. He is struggling to lift a wooden horse into its place. Two of the adults immediately run in to help. Before also joining in, the third uses his LG phone to tweet, "Restoring carousel. Come help." People see the Twitter update on their LG phones along with maps to the location and begin heading that way. The viewer sees people of different races, ages, and lifestyles working on the carousel and finally standing in wonder as the carousel lights up and begins spinning. It is a sweet, emotional scene showing that the phone doesn't just help with communication but with building community. The narration that closes the commercial says, "Is it a simple way to make a difference? The new LG Vortex: is it a smartphone or something better?"[12]

Advertisements can also promote a cause at the same time they promote a product. Examples include TOMS, BOMBAS, and Warby Parker. Each of these companies do well by doing good in that the model of these companies is to have consumers buy one of the products offered—shoes, socks, or eyeglasses, respectively—and then they give away one to a person in need.[13]

Finally, some of the best and most memorable ads appear as public service announcements (PSAs) without promoting a product at all. They raise awareness and teach about important social issues, critiquing destructive behavior and practices or offering models for good ones. The Ad Council is a nonprofit organization that has been around for more than seventy-five years and is the leader in spearheading such socially beneficial messages through advertising.[14] The ads are typically created pro bono by an advertising agency with media space in magazines and on television provided either free or at a greatly reduced cost. Some of the famous PSAs produced by the Ad

Council include topics related to Security of War Information with the campaign "Loose Lips Sink Ships" (1942–1945) or "Wild Fire Prevention with Smokey," to safety belt and polio education, AIDS prevention, and pollution: "Keep America Beautiful—Iron Eyes Cody."[15] Two fairly recent examples can highlight the power of such ads and show why advertising may have something to offer preachers.

First is an ad in which a middle-school-age girl steps out on stage to read an essay she has written during an assembly. The beginning looks sweet and innocent. The girl's essay is about Patty, who is shown in the audience. But then the essay shockingly begins speaking ill of Patty in short sentences calling her stupid, ugly, poor, and the like. At the end of the essay, words appear on screen with the clicklike sounds of a computer keyboard: "If you wouldn't say it in person, why say it online? Delete cyberbullying. Don't write it. Don't forward it." Then the words are highlighted as they might be on a computer screen and deleted with another sound of a keyboard click.[16] The message clearly illustrates the hurtful nature of cyberbullying and further suggests that people who pass along these types of messages, even if not the initial producer, are also doing wrong and should just delete texts that are intended to bully.

The second PSA begins with a shot of an older woman in her home surprised to hear a man outside performing a cheer that starts, "Oh those boys are much too much. Those boys are much too much." As the cheer continues with "We got the spirit!" the woman sees a large man through the window dancing, clapping, and wagging his finger. "We got the spirit! We're hot! We can't be stopped! We're gonna beat 'em!" After several seconds of this, the camera pans out to show what the woman cannot see: the man is practicing a cheer with his young cheerleader daughter. At that point, as the cheer continues, Tom Selleck begins a voiceover: "The smallest moments can have the biggest impact on a child's life." As the cheer concludes, Selleck starts up again, "Take time to be a dad today," and then we hear the father in the ad say, "One more time."[17]

CONCLUSION

Highlighting the best that advertising offers does not erase the fact that much advertising is involved in consumeristic, materialistic elements of human society that countercultural strains of the gospel seek to resist and reform. Nevertheless, the high points of advertising along with the effectiveness of the discipline in communicating its messages, embedding those messages in consumers' memories, and creating brand and value loyalty suggest it has lessons to teach preachers who strive to convey the gospel in a world in which communication must evolve to deal with the challenges of multimedia noise, postmodernism, and pluralism.

Both advertising and preaching are communicative endeavors aimed at persuading their audiences to consider new options for their lives. Without promoting material benefits and new options such as those that come from automobiles, televisions, shoes, and the like, preachers can still apply in their sermons advertising techniques to promote new life in Christ.

2

How Communication
Has Changed

What can preachers, who shape sermons (monological speeches that last anywhere from twelve to forty-five minutes), learn from the best of advertisers (who must communicate their message often in thirty seconds or less)? In attempting to answer this question, perhaps the best place to begin is with homiletics' and advertising's shared perspective concerning how communication works.

LINEAR COMMUNICATION

Modern advertising and modern homiletics have both been shaped by a linear model of communication. The primary understanding of such communication through the mid-twentieth century was sender-oriented and can be traced back to the early work of Shannon and Weaver in the late 1940s regarding the transmission of information.[1] The source or sender encodes a message by putting it into words or visual images and then delivers it through a certain channel or medium to be decoded or interpreted by the receiver, whose role is to then respond to the message. The traditional model allows for the sender to monitor responses through feedback efforts and takes into consideration "noise," such as other competing messages that might interrupt the message.[2]

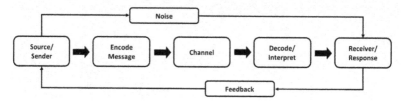

Figure 2.1   From Sandra Moriarty, Nancy Mitchell, Charles Wood, William Wells; *Advertising & IMC: Principles and Practice*, 11th Ed., ©2019.
Reprinted by permission of Pearson Education, Inc.

Two related assumptions serve as the foundation for this approach. First is the assumption that if the sender does the work of shaping the message well, the receiver will be able to decode the message easily, be appropriately impacted by the message, and be able to respond accordingly. In other words, properly formed content should correctly convey the information the communicator intended. This assumption is built on the idea that the sender and receiver come from similar cultural backgrounds and experiences, allowing for messages to be decoded as the sender intended.

Second, this linear communication model assumes that the sender has authority to communicate the intended message, and therefore the receiver grants the message itself authority. This assumption of communicative authority was widespread in the mid-twentieth century.

Consider journalism of that era. Many Americans trusted Walter Cronkite more than anyone else in the United States during his tenure as anchor of the *CBS Evening News* from 1962 to 1981. He delivered the news with a matter-of-fact posture and ended each broadcast with the tagline, "And that's the way it is." The line implies the news offered was given objectively and thus was the authoritative narration of the events of the day. Cronkite said it, I believe it, and that settles it. Education operated in much the same fashion. The teacher ruled the classroom with authority, delivering information for students to memorize and digest. Communication in the doctor's office followed this model as well. Physicians in their lab coats declared diagnoses, and patients followed their directions without questioning. While these three examples may be a bit exaggerated and there were certainly exceptions to the rule, they well illustrate the way communication functioned, or was thought to function, in a linear fashion.

Advertising of the period followed this model. Experts, or expert-sounding spokespersons—which for the era usually meant men—presented informational advertisements that authoritatively named the desirable benefits of a specific product. One example is a 1953 television commercial for Instant Maxwell House. Rex Marshall, a well-known television and radio personality of the period, was the spokesperson. After introducing the product, he contrasts it to others that he asserts are less desirable: Instant Maxwell House is not a powder or a grind, but "millions of tiny flavor buds of real coffee." He even places a spoonful of the product under a handheld microscope so that viewers can see the "hollow beads" up close. Marshall then describes the simple process for making the instant coffee while a faceless woman follows his directions. The commercial ends with Marshall inviting the viewers to "taste it" and presenting evidence of its desirability by claiming (without proof) that Instant Maxwell House is "preferred by more people across the country than any other instant coffee."[3] The ad is sender-oriented and assumes that communication moves in a simple linear fashion from sender to receiver and should be effective because the message is encoded in a way that conveys authoritative information about the nature of the product, how the product is used, and the popularity of the product. This mode of communication was presumed to make advertising persuasive.

Preaching in the mid-twentieth century utilized the same linear communication model. Actually, this model had been central to homiletics from a much earlier date. In 1870, John Albert Broadus published *A Treatise on the Preparation and Delivery of Sermons*. It, and later revisions by other scholars, would serve as the primary introductory homiletics textbook throughout U.S. seminaries for the better part of a century.[4] While the work draws on the classical rhetoric of Aristotle, Cicero, and Quintilian instead of using the terminology of communication studies, the sender-oriented approach is central. It is the preacher's job to appropriately interpret a biblical text (hermeneutics), build an argument conveying a message made up of logical parts (invention and arrangement), and deliver the message effectively (eloquence). The homiletical method focuses on content offered by an authoritative preacher and received by a hospitable audience or congregation.

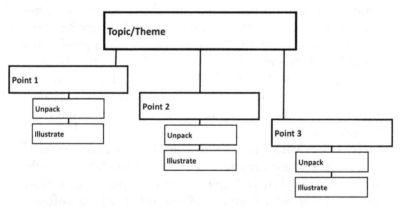

Figure 2.2

The result of this approach is the familiar (and still used) deductive, three-point sort of sermon. The preacher distills from a biblical text (be it narrative, poetry, prophecy, or epistle) a central proposition, which he (and the vast majority of preachers from this era would have been men) then breaks into smaller elements or "points." He organizes the points logically, involving exposition and illustration for persuasive effect.

MULTIDIRECTIONAL COMMUNICATION

A linear model of communication is less effective in the late twentieth and early twenty-first century than it had been in earlier days. The rise of technology, postmodernism, and pluralism mentioned earlier has shifted much of the authority in a communication event from the sender to the receiver. Part of this dynamic involves the fact that we live in an information age in which technology puts information at nearly everyone's fingertips. Anyone with a computer, tablet, or smartphone can immediately access huge amounts of information and competing truth claims from around the globe as well as having the ability to produce and publish such information at one's whim. The receiver in the linear model can now be the creator of content and the source of information that must be listened to if a relationship is to ensue between the two parties.

Further, communication theorists and practitioners recognize that the receiver doesn't simply passively receive communication from a sender or even solely decode a message as a sender intended. Receivers make meaning of the content communicated to them instead of simply accepting and being persuaded by it.

The result is that communication, specifically communication aimed at persuasion and meaning-making, moves in more than one direction. One way of visualizing this more complex communication model is to see it as cyclical, as Figure 2.3 (p. 18) shows.[5]

In this model, the communicator at the top of the diagram initiates the encoding of a message that is decoded, interpreted, and made into meaning by the initial receiver, who becomes the second communicator. The receiver/second communicator then in turn encodes feedback as a message to the first communicator, who must now receive, decode, interpret, and make meaning of that message. The communication evolves throughout the cycle.

The simple loop in the diagram belies the complexity of this model. As more communicators and channels are added, messages, feedback, encoding, and decoding move in multiple, overlapping, and even conflicting directions. No longer does

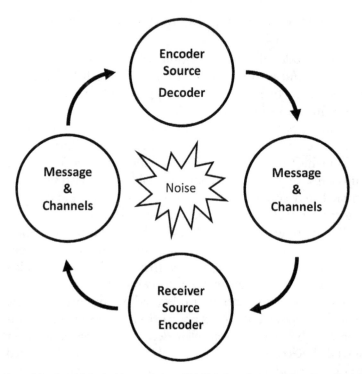

Figure 2.3   Republished with permission of SAGE College, [adapted] from Tom Altstiel and Jean Grow, *Advertising Creative: Strategy, Copy, and Design*, 4th ed., 2019; permission conveyed through Copyright Clearance Center, Inc.

some expert own the message and simply deliver it to a receptive audience. In today's world, audiences must be engaged as participants and co-creators of meaning if they are going to take communication initially directed to them seriously and build a relationship with communicators.

Let's return to the three cases we used to exemplify linear communication above. First, journalism: while there are still newscasts as well as print and online publications that strive to narrate the news as objectively as possible in a linear fashion to a receptive audience, they are the exceptions to the rule. In a world of twenty-four-hour news coverage, commentary has overtaken reporting. But the audience generally grants authority to those commentators with whom they agree and withholds authority from those with whom they disagree. For example, people with a more progressive political worldview tend to watch and agree with MSNBC while those with more conservative stances tend to watch and agree with Fox News. More than that, audiences engage figures in the news, journalistic celebrities, and the stories on which these celebrities comment through social media, call-in radio shows, and comment threads on online stories. And now, more and more often, news outlets are in turn reporting on what people are saying in these venues, showing Twitter comments and Facebook memes on the television screen. The multidirectional communication *about* a news story often becomes the news story itself.

Similarly in education, teachers now often think of themselves as co-learners with their students. Teachers' training and experience certainly give them some level of expertise in a subject matter but not the ultimate authority in determining the importance of the subject matter for students. Supposed objective, deductive, top-down lecturing has given way to subjective, inductive, conversational pedagogies. In this view, education is more than disseminating knowledge; it is empowering, liberating, and potentially political. The critical pedagogical proposals by authors such as Paulo Freire and bell hooks have been influential in this turn.[6]

In the doctor's office, communication has also become more complicated. While some patients, especially those of older generations, still take their physician at their word, more and more patients are engaged consumers. Armed with easily accessed information from WebMD, Wikipedia, and pharmaceutical ads, patients self-diagnose, request specific medications and treatments, and argue with their doctors. Patients now see themselves as consumers in conversation with medical experts but who must make choices for themselves about their own well-being. The days of a lab coat granting unquestionable authority are long gone.

People across domains want to have a voice and to be a part of the communication process. The result in advertising is that the old form of presenting a product, naming its benefits, and telling a consumer where to buy it within a thirty-second spot is no longer effective. Too many similar products are on the market, and multiple media outlets are seeking consumers' attention. Moreover, products are no longer purchased only for their functional benefits. Advertisers today need to seek a relationship with consumers by learning about consumers' needs and desires while listening to why, how, when, and where they want these fulfilled. Consumers want to create messages about brands they like and share these messages with their social networks. In order for this to happen, advertisers need to be on the same page as the consumers, using this consumer-generated information to enhance the value of their brands in the minds of those and other consumers. Market research is a critical component for advertisers to learn how to engage consumers and have them invite brands into their life stories.

One of the first, most radical, well-known, and successful examples of advertisers embracing a cyclical approach to communication and selling products was by Doritos. The company challenged consumers to produce an ad that would air during the most expensive advertising space of the year, the Super Bowl. The first contest was in 2007 and has become an annual event, encouraging user-generated content (UGC) for subsequent Super Bowl ads. The winning ad in 2007 was clever and highlighted different adjectives to describe Nacho Cheese Doritos. A man is driving in a parking lot eating a bag of Doritos when he sees a beautiful woman walking nearby also eating Doritos. The camera zooms in on the woman with the word "spicy" being displayed on screen. She sees the man in the car, and he makes an awkward smile in her direction while holding the bag of Doritos to be seen with the word "cheesy" appearing on screen. Not paying attention, the man rear-ends a car stopped in front of him. His face plows forward, crushing the Doritos into the steering wheel with the word "crunchy" on screen. The woman is concerned and braves oncoming traffic to run toward the car to check on the man, as the word "bold" appears on screen. Just as she is about to reach the car, "smooth?" appears on screen, and the woman trips and falls clumsily, bursting her bag of Doritos on the ground. Then the tagline for the ad appears: "Live the flavor."[7]

Homiletics has also responded to this cultural shift toward multidirectional and receiver-oriented communication models. Many preachers have laid aside Broadus's focus on content and the construction of a logical, persuasive, authoritative argument. In the late 1960s, many preachers experimented with "dialogue sermons" in which two preachers ping-ponged back and forth between each other to deliver the sermon, or a lone preacher would engage in a give-and-take with the congregation.[8] Neither of these approaches were influential in the long run, partly because the approaches did not fit well in a liturgical context and partly because the "dialogue" was necessarily contrived. In the 1970s, however, the New Homiletic stepped onto the scene. Scholars of this movement sought approaches that embodied the receiver-oriented principles of dialogue sermons while remaining monologues in form. Indeed the movement has often been described as a turn to the listener. Fred B. Craddock's *As One without Authority* sounded the bugle call for such a shift.[9] Craddock turned Broadus's work on its head, arguing that after centuries of deductive sermons, preachers should engage in inductive preaching. Instead of declaring one's propositional message and breaking it into points, Craddock argued that preachers should take hearers on a journey through the biblical text, connecting it with the details of contemporary life along the way. The sermon ends, not with the preacher "applying" it to what the congregation should do, but in an open-ended fashion, empowering the hearers to determine the conclusion for themselves.

In recent years, some homiletical scholars have moved beyond the New Homiletic in attempting to offer an even stronger role and higher level of authority to the congregation in the sermonic event. The result is a collaborative-conversational school of homiletics.[10]

John S. McClure proposes a method of preparing sermons in which a group from the congregation gathers during the week to discuss the biblical text and its meaning for contemporary life. The preacher does not control the group but instead acts as its steward, as both host and guest, speaker and listener. In the sermon on Sunday, the preacher then offers a monological sermon that conveys and builds on the dynamics of that weekday conversation.[11]

Lucy Atkinson Rose proposes a feminist theology of preaching in which the goal of the sermon is to gather the congregation, week after week, around the Word, where the central conversations of the church are refocused and fostered. Sermons offer tentative proposals concerning the interpretations of an ancient biblical text and of God in the world today to create space for genuine conversations that could involve counterproposals.[12]

Ronald J. Allen argues for bringing different voices into the sermon—such as the Bible, Christian history and tradition, contemporary theologians, the wider world, the life of the congregation, and the life of the preacher. These voices may agree at points and disagree at others, offering the congregation resources for determining on their own what makes for an adequate theological interpretation of life and the world.[13]

O. Wesley Allen, Jr. views the church as a matrix of conversations in which individuals and the community of faith strive to make meaning of the world (and all the various aspects of life) through a Christian lens. The preacher is a privileged voice in that conversation (getting to speak a monologue before the whole assembly week after week), but neither initiates nor has the final, definitive word in the conversation. While all participants in the conversation have access to reason and experience, the preacher's primary role is to bring Scripture and tradition into the conversation, since the preacher has been set apart by the church to study these on behalf of the church. The presentation of Scripture and tradition supplies the vocabulary of the conversation.[14]

These examples show that homiletics has been observing some of the same shifts in the communication environment as advertising. Advertising and preaching have both been seeking ways to communicate that are appropriate to and effective for our postmodern era. The move from approaching communication using a linear model to an approach appreciating a multidirectional understanding of communication invites consumers of ads and hearers of sermons to make meaning in conversation with the message offered as both decoder and encoder instead of simply as a passive receiver. The communicative situation in which we find ourselves and the audiences in this situation are complex. It should not be taken for granted that we preachers naturally or intuitively know how to communicate best in this situation or even to whom we are communicating. In the next chapter, we turn to techniques that advertising uses to better understand its target markets in order to rethink some of the ways we preachers can get a better handle on the hearers to whom we offer the gospel.

3

Understanding the Hearer

Every week, we preachers sit down in our studies and begin our sermon preparation asking (explicitly or implicitly) something like, *What is the most significant aspect or experience of God's presence in the world and its implications to which I can witness through this particular biblical text in conversation with this particular community of faith on this particular occasion?*

"Particular biblical text." "Particular community of faith." "Particular occasion." Attending to the particularities in the preaching event can make the difference between an average sermon that is quickly forgotten and one that claims the listeners as a timely and existential message that has the potential to transform the listener. In this chapter we are concerned with the particularities of the congregation—the community of faith.

Preachers do not prepare sermons in a vacuum. To an outsider, it may look like preachers sit in their studies alone working on their sermons. But preachers know that as they sit at their desks interpreting a biblical text, pouring over commentaries, shaping a central message, determining the rhetorical flow of the sermon, searching for sermonic imagery, and drafting a manuscript or notes, members of their congregation are all around. Congregants stand next to them tapping them on the arm, sit on their shoulders whispering in their ears, and stand across the room throwing wadded pieces of paper at them to get the preacher's attention. They remind preachers of the values they most deeply hold, the personal struggles happening in their lives, the news items that worry them, their celebrations at school or work, doubts they have about certain elements of Christian faith, and elements of the Christian faith about which they feel certain. Preachers do not address generic congregations, so they should not preach generic sermons.

Through their lives with the community of faith, pastors get to know their flock organically and intuitively. Hospital and home visits, study groups, counseling sessions, committee meetings, and the like all provide preachers with the chance to learn things about their listeners. While this process is natural, healthy, and good, we must be careful to find ways to move to deeper and more critical understandings of the joys, theologies, political ideologies, concerns, and sufferings of our hearers. Too often we get comfortable with our view of the congregation, and our sermons end up targeting a construct that is no longer as close to the reality of our flock as it ought to be.

Marketers often find themselves in similar situations where a once-strong brand slowly and over time loses a significant amount of market share due to misperceiving the changing market. In the 1980s, Lean Cuisine was a brand riding high as a product for people interested in weight loss and dieting. By 2015, however, the brand had experienced five years of significantly declining sales.[1] After undertaking research and listening to consumers, Lean Cuisine found it had become irrelevant to consumers who had moved on from dieting and now wanted to focus on living healthy lifestyles. The research showed that consumers perceived Lean Cuisine as a quick-fix meal for lonely and dieting single women and that consumers were actually embarrassed to be seen purchasing Lean Cuisine at the checkout. With this information, Lean Cuisine shifted its communication focus from dieting to being an advocate for female empowerment, health, and wellness. They dropped the word "diet" from all marketing communication, redesigned packaging to be more modern, and sought out stories for its commercials of how women felt accomplished in their lives outside of weight and their bodies. Lean Cuisine positioned itself alongside healthy and accomplished women to "feed what really matters to you," engaging real women to share their stories online. Sales increased the next year by $56 million.[2]

In addition to addressing declining market shares, advertising agencies engage in research regarding the brand, the market, and consumers in order to develop new objectives, segment the market, and develop effective communication that resonates with the target audience. Advertisers use a variety of techniques—from secondary research, such as looking at existing demographic data for help in segmenting the market, and first-hand research such as surveys, interviews, and focus groups—to better understand consumer attitudes, motivations, preferences, and behaviors. Preachers do not have such primary tools available to them to better understand their congregations, but they can adapt some basic techniques of secondary market research to help continually deepen and renew insights into their congregations and incorporate from these insights what people in the pews need from sermons.

MARKET SEGMENTATION

Consider a person's circle of friends. Each friend is different, and the person's relationship with each one is different. One friend might be a sounding board and confidant, another a travel companion, and yet another is great for financial advice. Different friends serve different needs at different times.

Consumers experience brands in a similar way. Consumers have a seemingly infinite variety of desires and needs, and no product, service, or message is universally attractive. Moreover, one brand fulfills one type of need for one person and a different desire for another. For example, consumers go to some brands for functional or psychological benefits. A *functional benefit* is the utility received from simply using the product to fix a tangible problem. For example, some people buy toothpaste simply to prevent cavities. A *psychological benefit*, on the other hand, is derived from a brand providing feelings of happiness, joy, fitting in, confidence, or being tied to one's self-identity. Returning to toothpaste, some feel more confident after having used the whitening power of toothpaste because they were seeking to enhance their self-esteem in relation to appearance or wanting to fit in socially with other friends who have white teeth.

The purchase of an automobile can be viewed in the same way. Some people buy a car for getting from point A to point B in the cheapest way possible. Such consumers look at price, reliability, and gas mileage when purchasing a vehicle. They are simply seeking to have a functional need fulfilled and might purchase an economy model such as a Ford Focus. In contrast, consumers who experience their cars as extensions of their identities may spend more on a car that can provide the psychological image the person is seeking to project, such as the economic status conveyed by a Mercedes-Benz Cabriolet convertible or concern for the environment addressed by a hybrid such as a Toyota Prius.

In order to attract a particular group of consumers, advertisers tailor the presentation of their brand to that group's particular shared needs and desires. Sometimes such tailoring requires research to determine what those needs and desires are (as in the earlier case of rebranding Lean Cuisine). Often, however, such research is not required or possible. Instead, advertisers use already available secondary data that describes characteristics of different population groups. Examining this data allows advertisers to develop an understanding of the needs and wants of large population groups in order to create messages that will be meaningful to a particular group. This process is called *market segmentation*.

A potential market can be divided, or segmented, in a variety of ways. Researchers have created and published various useful taxonomies of consumers based on a number of different characteristics—such as geographic location, demographic factors, behavioristic patterns, and psychographic values—in order to identify consumers whom they believe will be responsive to their products. Let's examine some of these different segmentations that may be of use to preachers.

First, *geographic segmentation* has to do with understanding people based on location, which could be defined by country, region of the country, or even very locally, as in a neighborhood. Populations of geographical regions often have unique cultural practices and values, including things like shared or similar religion, food tastes, etiquette, commerce, benefits, struggles, and the like.

As an example, global marketers use lists of value rankings that differ by country, often based on historical and cultural factors.[3] Compare the differences in the top values of the United States, Belgium, and China:

United States	Belgium	China
Freedom	Owning one's own	Obedience
Equality in law	house	Being hardworking
Equality in	Thriftiness	Tolerance of others
opportunity	Descendants	Harmony with
Fairness	Health	others
Achievement	Safety	Humbleness
Patriotism	Security	Loyalty
Democracy		Respect for rituals

Companies that want to sell their products in these different countries must rely on advertising companies to position those products differently in the different countries and cultures. An ad that is attractive to Belgian consumers might turn off U.S. or Chinese consumers.

Several different online resources provide information for examining values and beliefs by country. *Hofstede Insights* is a website providing country-specific values across six dimensions:[4]

- **Power Distance Index.** This dimension expresses the degree to which the less powerful members of a society accept and expect that power is distributed unequally.

- **Individualism versus collectivism.** *Individualism* can be defined as a preference for a loosely knit social framework in which individuals are expected to take care of only themselves and their immediate families, while *collectivism* represents a preference for a tightly knit framework in society in which individuals can expect their relatives or members of a particular in-group to look after them in exchange for unquestioning loyalty.

- **Masculinity versus femininity.** The masculine side of this dimension represents a preference in a competitive society for achievement, heroism, assertiveness, and material rewards for success. Its opposite, femininity, stands for a preference for a more consensus-based society with focuses such as cooperation, modesty, caring for the weak, and quality of life.

- **Uncertainty Avoidance Index.** The Uncertainty Avoidance dimension expresses the degree to which the members of a society feel uncomfortable with uncertainty and ambiguity—whether a society tries to control the future or just let it happen.

- **Long-term orientation versus short-term normative orientation.** Societies with a long-term orientation prefer to maintain time-honored traditions and norms while viewing societal change with suspicion. Cultures with a short-term orientation take a more pragmatic approach, encouraging thrift and efforts in modern education as a way to prepare for the future.

- **Indulgence versus restraint.** Indulgence stands for a society that allows relatively free gratification of basic and natural human drives related to enjoying life and having fun. Restraint stands for a society that suppresses gratification of needs and regulates it by means of strict social norms.

Advertisers can use knowledge about a culture's dominant values to better understand the best messaging to reach consumers in different countries. For example, a country or target audience that is more individualistic could be considered more favorable to advertising messages focused on the unique individual and being the "best *you* can be." In contrast, more collectivistic cultures may prefer messages focused on group dynamics and being the "best *we* can be." A revealing case study of how this occurs is the Sony Walkman, the individual portable music device that was first released in 1979. The product was a great success in both the United States and Japan. Its appeal in the two cultures, however, was quite different. In the United States, an individualistic culture, Sony marketed the product as allowing consumers to hear their music without being bothered by others. However, in Japan, a more collectivistic culture, Sony marketed the Walkman as allowing consumers to listen to their music without bothering others.[5]

A second example of market segmentation is *demographic segmentation*, which compares and contrasts variables across age, gender, family size, life cycle, income, occupation, education, race, ethnicity, and religion. Populations within a demographic group often share similar ranges of values, concerns, and life experiences. In the United States, there are differences in key characteristics between the generations.[6]

TRADITIONALISTS	BOOMERS	GEN X	MILLENNIALS	GEN 2020
Born 1900–1945	Born 1946–1964	Born 1965–1976	Born 1977–1997	Born after 1997
Great Depression World War II Disciplined Workplace loyalty Move to the suburbs Vaccines Television	Vietnam Moon landing Civil/women's rights Experimental Innovators Hard-working Personal computer	Fall of Berlin Wall Gulf War Independent Free agents AIDS Internet, MTV Mobile phone	9/11 attacks Community service Immediacy Confident Diversity Google, Facebook Tablets	Optimistic High expectations Apps Social games Smartphones

When developing messages for baby boomers born between 1946 and 1964 and growing up during the civil rights and women's movements, advertising focused on fulfilling one's potential is often effective. One scholar suggests that AARP's messaging—with phrases such as "Life Reimagined" or "You've Still Got It"—are good examples to reach this group. In contrast, Millennials are motivated to make a wider difference in the world while Generation Xers are skeptics and need assurance about the trustworthiness of messages and brands.[7]

Overall, any particular advertising approach is perceived differently by these varied generations, and understanding the general differences in order to develop effective messages is important. Nike found this out with its advertisement celebrating thirty years of the "Just Do It" campaign. Nike used the former San Francisco 49ers quarterback Colin Kaepernick to narrate and appear in a two-minute ad titled "Dream Crazy."[8] The choice of Kaepernick was controversial because he was at the center of a cultural fight concerning race and patriotism. In 2016 he began a movement of athletes refusing to stand during the national anthem at an NFL game to protest injustices in society against African Americans and other people of color.[9] Many, however, saw the action as unpatriotic and claimed it was disrespectful to those in military service. President Donald Trump weighed in on Twitter, saying NFL owners should fire athletes refusing to stand. After the 2017 season Kaepernick opted out of his contract with the 49ers to become a free agent but was not signed by any other team in spite of the fact that he had led San Francisco to a Super Bowl appearance in 2012 and an NFC championship game in 2013. He filed a lawsuit against the NFL owners for colluding to keep him out of the sport, which resulted in a confidential settlement.

Morning Consult, a global marketing research firm, conducted a study in which they asked two thousand people to watch the two-minute Nike ad and continually rate their engagement and appreciation of the ad by turning a hand dial to higher and lower values (a common technique for analyzing the effectiveness of advertising).[10] The Nike ad shows more than twenty athletes (including children, youth, unknown adults, and celebrities) overcoming significant hurdles to become great in their sport while Kaepernick's unidentified voice narrates the script. Appreciation for the ad is high and rises across all generational demographics measured for the first three-fifths of the ad. However, when Kaepernick first appears on screen around the one-minute, twenty-second mark with the narration, "Believe in something, even if it means sacrificing everything," a significant generational divide occurs. Viewers ages eighteen to thirty-seven continue with a high appreciation of the ad, but thirty-eight- to seventy-two-year-old viewers' appreciation drops considerably. It drops for these same groups again at the end of the ad when Kaepernick reappears on screen and says, "So don't ask if your dreams are crazy. Ask if they are crazy enough."

A third type of market segmentation, *behavioristic segmentation*, focuses on action or inaction—in what ways and how frequently people use a brand. Advertisers typically subgroup consumer behavior according to amount of use (light, moderate, and heavy users), time of day that products are used, and what benefits are perceived for each group. Cereal is a great example of a category with which advertisers have used behavioristic segmentation combined with generational segmentation to better target ads that would increase consumer occasions of using the product. Cereal used to be just a breakfast food, but today it is expanding into the snack-food category. Concern over sugared cereal to start one's day has made room for healthier cereals to be eaten in the morning, with sugared cereals as tasty snacks anytime. In fact, a report by Mintel indicates that 43 percent of people in the United States are eating cereal as a snack, with 53 percent of Millennials and 33 percent of baby boomers driving the change. Interestingly, cereals desired as snacks are the more sugar-laden options such as Froot Loops and Lucky Charms, allowing sales of these types to continue while expanding the overall cereal market from breakfast to all day and anytime.[11]

While demographic segmentation is helpful, it has significant limitations. On the one hand, advertisers cannot assume everyone in a particular demographic segment shares the same values, interests, attitudes, and behaviors. On the other hand, products are often purchased by people who fit in multiple demographic categories, and advertisers want to expand the sphere of their brand as much as possible. One way of dealing with these shortcomings is to draw on a fourth way of segmenting the population: psychographic segmentation. *Psychographic segmentation* divides the potential market for a product based on shared lifestyles, personalities, attitudes, and values that may cross over geographic, demographic, and behavioristic variables.

Let's take values as a particular example of a psychographic factor to assess in understanding people, learning what motivates them, and creating personally relevant messages. With "values," advertisers are concerned with enduring beliefs that motivate behavior and cause us to prefer one choice over another.[12] Advertising and market research firms spend considerable amounts of time and money gathering information on values their consumers hold. One company, Strategic Business Insights, combines research on values, attitudes, and lifestyles (VALS) to identify eight segments of values categories based on people's primary motivation and resources:[13]

Innovators	Thinkers
• Are always taking in information (antennas up) • Are confident enough to experiment • Make the highest number of financial transactions • Are skeptical about advertising • Have international exposure • Are future-oriented • Are self-directed consumers • Believe science and R&D are credible	• Have "ought" and "should" benchmarks for social conduct • Have a tendency toward analysis paralysis • Plan, research, and consider before they act • Enjoy a historical perspective • Are financially established • Are not influenced by what's hot • Use technology in functional ways

• Are most receptive to new ideas and technologies • Enjoy the challenge of problem solving • Have the widest variety of interests and activities	• Prefer traditional intellectual pursuits • Buy proven products
Believers	**Achievers**
• Believe in basic rights and wrongs to lead a good life • Rely on spirituality and faith to provide inspiration • Want friendly communities • Watch TV and read romance novels to find an escape • Want to know where things stand; have no tolerance for ambiguity • Are not looking to change society • Find advertising a legitimate source of information • Value constancy and stability (can appear to be loyal) • Have strong me-too fashion attitudes	• Have a "me first, my family first" attitude • Believe money is the source of authority • Are committed to family and job • Are fully scheduled • Are goal-oriented • Are hardworking • Are moderate • Act as anchors of the status quo • Are peer-conscious • Are private • Are professional • Value technology that provides a productivity boost
Strivers	**Experiencers**
• Have revolving employment; high temporary unemployment • Use video and video games as a form of fantasy • Are fun-loving • Are imitative • Rely heavily on public transportation • Are the center of low-status street culture	• Want everything • Are first in and first out of trend adoption • Go against the current mainstream • Are up on the latest fashions • Love physical activity (are sensation seeking) • See themselves as very sociable • Believe that friends are extremely important

continued on next page

• Desire to better their lives but have difficulty in realizing their desire • Wear their wealth	• Are spontaneous • Have a heightened sense of visual stimulation
Makers	**Survivors**
• Are distrustful of government • Have a strong interest in all things automotive • Have strong outdoor interests (hunting and fishing) • Believe in sharp gender roles • Want to protect what they perceive to be theirs • See themselves as straight-forward; appear to others as anti-intellectual • Want to own land	• Are cautious and risk averse • Are the oldest consumers • Are thrifty • Are not concerned about appearing traditional or trendy • Take comfort in routine, familiar people and places • Are heavy TV viewers • Are loyal to brands and products • Spend most of their time alone • Are the least likely to use the Internet • Are the most likely to have a landline-only household

Advertisers can tailor different messages to market their brands to different VALS types. For example, if the target for a message is in the Thinker group, the message needs to provide arguments and facts to help the recipient want to engage with the ideas. In contrast, people from the Experiencers group may do fine with the general message offered to Thinkers, but they will want some type of action associated with the message to actually experience the concept. David Sleeth-Keppler provides two different examples of how to employ VALS in positioning products, using Nutella Hazelnut Spread as an example.[14] He describes the target for Nutella as busy moms who are Achievers looking for something nutritious to feed their children in the morning but easy enough to get them out the door and off to school on time. Sleeth-Keppler explains that the benefits of the product to this psychographic target are its convenience, nutritional value, and appeal to children. As another example,

Sleeth-Keppler argues that the GoPro camera is positioned as a substitute to regular digital cameras and the target for the product from the VALS list are Experiencers: spontaneous people who seek adventure and like elevated visual stimulation. He describes the main benefit to this target audience as someone feeling like an action hero.

CONGREGATIONAL SEGMENTATION

Homiletics has not traditionally concerned itself specifically with market research, but some scholars have helped preachers better understand their hearers so that their sermons are fitting for their particular congregational context. Lenora Tubbs Tisdale and James R. Nieman draw on ethnographic approaches for exegeting the congregations.[15] Matthew D. Kim uses methods from studies in cultural intelligence to help preachers more effectively speak to their specific hearers.[16]

More narrowly, homiletics has not drawn on market segmentation, but studies have attempted to deal with diverse groups in the congregation. James R. Nieman and Thomas G. Rogers deal with preaching in a culturally diverse congregation.[17] Joseph R. Jeter and Ronald J. Allen also address preaching across a range of demographic differences in the same congregation.[18] Thomas H. Troeger and H. Edward Everding Jr. present homiletical approaches for preaching to a congregation comprising people with different intelligences and learning styles.[19] Most recently, Leah D. Schade has written about preaching in the midst of the political division in U.S. culture and in individual congregations.[20]

In truth, more than consciously employing the various methods proposed by these different homiletical scholars, most pastors exegete their congregations intuitively. Ask any pastor about their congregation, and they can quickly and easily give a rundown of the basic age span, racial composition, educational level, theological and political leanings, and pastoral concerns of their flock. Pastors study those in their care whenever they are with them—in youth group, choir rehearsal, appointments in the office, finance committee, fellowship events, hospital calls, or accidental meetings in the grocery store.

Preachers, however, face two common problems in developing a picture of their congregation through this sort of intuitive study. First, we tend to be reductionistic in interpretations of our congregations. We smooth over the edges of diversity and division, looking for the members' commonalities. This is natural given that something clearly binds any particular congregation together. And this approach is useful: we must minister and preach to the whole, and creating a construct of our congregation based on a sense of homogeneity that stretches across generational, behavioristic, and psychographic differences allows us to do so. After all, a congregation is filled with people who have varied needs and worries, and a multitude of characteristics. Knowing every person intimately and meeting the individual needs of each one every week with a sermon is impossible. The problem, of course, is that—more often than not—we may be preaching to a construct of our people that is not as useful or precise as it might be.

This leads to the second problem: our construct of our congregation may not just be reductionistic, it may be wrong. Similar to the Lean Cuisine brand, we may be preaching to people based on a particular image of their needs and desires while they actually have moved beyond the image we hold.

Pastors may be too close to their congregation to see fully the people to whom they minister. True, we are invited into parts of our parishioners' lives that few others see. But it is also true that congregants hide significant parts of themselves from their pastors' view. Thus, we must seek tools to help us understand congregants in their diversity that they themselves may not be willing to share with us or of which they are not even consciously aware. Using secondary tools of market segmentation with our congregations can be such a resource. Certainly, segmentation still leads to the creation of a reductionistic construction to which to preach, but it can expand our current construct based on data of widespread patterns. Segmentation can help us view the congregation as a compilation of groups (instead of individuals) with diverse needs and desires.

Geographic segmentation may offer little help for a preacher of a congregation where almost everyone has lived their whole life in the same locale in which they worship. But if a church attracts people from a variety of different national or cultural backgrounds—where people share the benefits, difficulties, and feelings of having been transplanted from family and friends—learning about values of different geographic regions represented in the congregation can be quite helpful. Also, many pastors are called to churches outside their geographic region of origin. In such situations, a pastor can use geographic segmentation to help understand differences that exist between the preacher's own experiences and values and those of the congregation and then better bridge those differences.

Demographic segmentation is perhaps the most familiar form of segmentation to many preachers, and for good reason. It can be quite helpful in that preachers can look for some demographic commonalities over against other demographic differences in the community of faith. A church may have generational diversity but share an ethnic background. Preachers can try to connect with the congregation by drawing on those characteristics that are similar to each other and use these factors in sermons. On the other hand, demographic segmentation can help preachers see diversity where they have missed it. Preachers of smaller churches often have primarily older people in their congregations. This can lead to a monolithic view of their needs and values. But demographic segmentation can help preachers see differences even between traditionalists (born before 1946) and baby boomers (born 1946–1964).

Behavioristic segmentation can lead preachers to see the different ways worshipers approach Christian faith broadly and listen to sermons more narrowly based on where they fall on a scale of active participation in church life and worship attendance. Sermon series are currently popular among preachers. A series extending over six weeks, however, is received differently by a congregant who is in attendance every week versus one who comes to worship on the second and fifth Sundays of the series, much less by a first-time visitor who shows up on the third Sunday of the series.

Psychographic segmentation can lead preachers to view the composition of their congregation in still different ways. Many pastors have long been familiar with the Myers-Briggs personality types and have used them to better understand themselves and their congregants.[21] Some are now becoming interested in Enneagram personality types for the same reasons.[22] Using the categorization of people by values can add to these types of perspectives. Strategic Business Insights offers an online survey through which participants can find out in which VALS type they fit.[23] It would be an easy and interesting experiment for preachers to ask a cross section of their congregation to take the online survey and collect the results. Knowing what VALS types are attracted to this congregation would help preachers create sermons that are relevant to these people's values, motivation, lifestyles, and available resources.

While preachers can use segmentation to recognize that more diversity is present among their hearers than they had imagined, this realization can also be overwhelming. How in the world can a preacher effectively address all of the congregational segments in a single sermon? How are we to preach to those who grew up in the southern United States and immigrants from sub-Saharan Africa (geographic), Gen Xers and Millennials (demographic), longtime members and seekers (behavioristic), and those who jump on every trend and those who are averse to risk (psychographic), all at the same time? After all, advertising has the luxury of shaping specific ads for specifically narrow segments of the consumer population, but preachers must address their sermons to everyone who shows up on Sunday morning. It would be unfaithful to the task of proclaiming God's word to preach this week to this segment of the congregation and next week to another, and so on and so forth. No, every Sunday all congregants show up hoping to receive a word from and about God for them. We preachers certainly miss the mark at times, but we should never intentionally aim away from some segment of the congregation, using the rationale that it better helps us speak to a different segment. While diverse, the body of Christ is not for the preacher to divide.

What is needed is a homiletical approach that offers a message to the whole while attending to the needs and interests of different segments in different parts of the sermon. To return to advertising for an analogy, advertisers often promote a brand with an umbrella message and then narrow that message for particular segments of the market in different ads. Consider Arm & Hammer Baking Soda. On the product's website the umbrella message is, "The small box with endless possibilities."[24] This broad tagline invites wide interest. The dropdown boxes on the site then offer different baking soda products for laundry, cat litter, oral care, and personal care. A review of the site reveals that the product is marketed for cooking, cleaning, and health purposes. Arm & Hammer can use data gathered from potential consumers' online searches and purchase histories to post particular ads for their baking soda on their social media threads. People who have purchased kitchen and food items might see ads focused on using Arm & Hammer in cooking and cleaning, while athletes who have searched for articles about muscle pain might see ads suggesting an Arm & Hammer Baking Soda bath.

Preachers can construct sermons in a similar fashion. The central message of the sermon functions like the umbrella message aimed at the whole congregation. Different parts of the sermon, especially different images and stories (see chapter 5) can be aimed to draw that message closer to different segments of hearers. Consider a sermon on the parable of the Prodigal Son (Luke 15:11–25). A preacher interested in attending to different congregational segments in a single sermon might think the best approach would be to invite different segments to identify with different characters in the parable—one segment with the father, another with the younger son, and still another with the elder son. Actually, though, this approach really leads to three mini-sermons and no umbrella message for the whole community of faith. A better approach is to determine which character in the parable will serve as the focus of the sermon and develop a central sermonic claim based on him. Then, to help hearers from different segments relate to the message based on that character, the preacher can draw on multiple contemporary images, metaphors, examples, and stories that connect different segments with the message from their perspective, experience, and values. In some stories, older characters are used and in

others younger. Some language is more appealing to Innova-
tors and other language to Survivors. Early in the sermon, an
example can be drawn from an intimate couple and later one
comes from the life of a single person. Some biblical and theological exposition is broad and accessible to seekers, and some is
deeper and appealing to those long committed to discipleship.

Preachers, however, can only go so far multiplying different segmental connections in a sermon without preaching for
three and a half hours. How is one to shape a sermon with
an umbrella message and segmented imagery that is realistic
and has real possibility of connecting diverse hearers with the
proclamation of God's good news? One way is to tighten the
preacher's focus on congregational diversity by learning from
the way advertisers use focus groups.

MARKET RESEARCH FOCUS GROUPS

Advertisers recognize that market segmentation, while valuable,
is limited. Targeting an audience based on broad data about a
certain segment or group of segments of consumers requires not
only making assumptions about their needs, desires, values, and
behavior, but also about how they will perceive a message aimed at
attracting them to a product. One approach advertisers use to try
to move beyond such assumptions is to test a message or ad with a
focus group, a qualitative method of research that advertisers use
to get a sense about how people explain the way they actually feel
about a product, brand, concept, or advertising campaign.

Typically, a *focus group* involves six to eight people who participate in a directed interview or discussion group led by a trained
moderator who works for the advertising agency. The moderator
asks questions to better understand the consumers' perspectives
on a brand or an advertising concept. Advertising agencies used
to conduct focus groups in person at a set location, but today
many companies also engage in online focus groups.

When conducting focus groups, moderators often use a useful technique of questioning the group called laddering, which

helps them reach something that otherwise would be out of reach.[25] Laddering is grounded in means-end chain theory, which argues that consumers make purchasing decisions based on a hierarchy of unconscious perceptions that relate to different levels of conscious consideration.[26] People buy features and benefits that satisfy emotions and beliefs, but they rationalize their purchase by focusing on functional benefits. Laddering is an interview technique that helps moderators begin with interviewees' surface-level rationales (usually expressed in terms of what someone "likes" about a product) to higher values they hold in relation to a product or brand (expressed in terms of how someone "feels" they benefit from a product). As seen in the following diagram, marketers assume that consumers hold a hierarchy of four core levels of considerations when choosing to purchase a product:

| **Value** |
| State of being that the consumer is trying to achieve |
| **Psychosocial Consequence** |
| Emotional benefits achieved by using the product |
| **Functional Consequence** |
| Immediate and tangible benefits achieved by using the product |
| **Attribute** |
| Tangible features of the product |

Figure 3.1   Republished with permission of Sage Publications Inc., [adapted] from American Marketing Association, American Marketing Society, National Association of Marketing Teachers; Jonathan Gutman, "A Means-End Chain Model Based on Consumer Categorization Processes," *Journal of Marketing*, vol. 46, no. 2, 1982; permission conveyed through Copyright Clearance Center, Inc.

The higher on the ladder an ad makes a connection with consumers, the more effective the ad will be; for example, ads that connect emotionally with consumers and give the message that a product will help them reach the state of being they desire are going to be more attractive than ones that simply name the functional benefits of a product.

When interviewing members of a focus group, laddering helps a moderator identify participants' motivations for using a product that may not be obvious with their initial response to an ad or product or initial answers to questions posed by the moderator. By using a series of questions building on each other, important pieces of information can be uncovered related to consumers' needs and wants. Specifically, this technique allows the researcher to find out what attributes (product features), benefits (functional or emotional), and values are most important to consumers regarding the product category.

According to Thomas Grubert, there are three core questions for laddering. The moderator starts with "Why did you choose this product/service?" This question elicits responses in which consumers name the attributes of a product that are important to them. Next the moderator asks, "Why is [that attribute] good/bad . . . ?" This question moves the interviewees from naming attributes to discussing benefits. The focus group participants may begin with functional benefits, but the moderator can lead them to discuss emotional benefits as well. These answers set up the final level of questions asking, "Why is this benefit important to you?" This query allows respondents to name the values they hold that are impacted by each consequence or benefit of the product's different attributes. In sum, the laddering technique allows the researcher to move from rational and easily accessible features and benefits to more abstract, emotional, and unconscious values.[27]

For an example at the brand level, consider Adidas workout clothing. In response to the first question of "Why did you choose this product?" the respondent might say, "I like the look of the clothing and that real athletes endorse the brand." The moderator would follow up with the second question:

"Why is it good that Adidas looks good and that real athletes endorse the brand?" The respondent answers, "The clothing looks like you are serious about working out and real athletes endorsing the brand make Adidas seem authentic." Finally, the moderator asks a question to get at the emotion and value connected to these ideas: "Why is looking serious about working out and using a brand that is authentic via real athletes important to you?" The respondent answers, "When I wear Adidas, I feel like a real athlete who is serious about keeping in good health, and it motivates me to keep improving to be like the real athletes using the brand." In moving through the laddering process we are able to identify and connect functional benefits with personal and often emotional value-driven end goals. Adidas-brand clothing leads to the emotional benefit of self-worth through an association as being counted among real athletes as well as providing inspiration to keep achieving a healthy life. While benefits vary for different groups of consumers, typically enough others fall in this same category of benefits so that targeted advertising messages can be developed. In this particular example, advertising copy could follow from these findings: "Be the best athlete you can be, getting the performance quality you need to keep rising up just like the pros, with X Brand workout wear."

CONGREGATIONAL SEGMENTATION INTO IMAGINATIVE FOCUS GROUPS

While some homileticians have suggested collaborative approaches to developing sermons,[28] most preachers would find it unrealistic to run weekly focus groups to sharpen a message or tweak the sermon imagery. Some preachers do this intuitively. One pastor goes into the worship space every week in the middle of sermon preparation. At this point he has done exegesis on his biblical text, shaped a draft of his central message, and started thinking about imagery he will use to fill out the sermon. He wanders around the nave and sits in different pews where specific parishioners sit. Then he asks himself, *What word from God does Bonnie need to hear this week?* and *How will Michael hear the message I am intending?* He then carries his ponderings about various parishioners back to the study with him as he sharpens his message, determines the flow of the sermon, and picks imagery to touch the lives of these hearers.

Preachers can follow this approach, combine it with lessons learned from market segmentation and research focus groups, and create an imaginative, empathetic focus group to use on a weekly basis. First, preachers should draw a floor plan of their worship space on a large piece of paper. Keep multiple photocopies of the floor plan on hand as templates to be used later.

Second, list six to nine parishioners on the floor plan where they usually sit. They should be spread across the worship space. List descriptors of these parishioners using the various types of segmentation listed above—geographic, demographic, behavioristic, and psychographic. Add notes concerning your general impression of their theological orientation or faith experience, as well as comments concerning anything that help them stand out as unique individuals. You might have something like Figure 3.2 for three of the individuals.

To flesh out more in the preacher's mind the members of the focus group, especially those with whom the preacher is less familiar, one could find a time to visit with them, share a meal, and get to know them better. Indeed, asking each person listed on the page a few of the same questions in the sense of an informal poll would assist the preacher in seeing both differences and similarities. Questions could relate to upcoming sermon series or themes of liturgical seasons.

The preacher, then, would use this group as an imaginary focus group while preparing a sermon. Empathizing with these specific individuals (stereotyped representatives of larger groups in the congregation, but also actual people with real faces for the preacher to see) each week can help preachers move their sermons from generic messages to the level of particularity that allows them to be their most effective. Using an imaginary

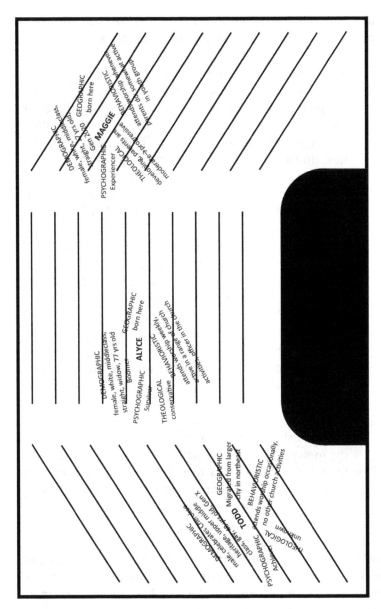

MAGGIE

DEMOGRAPHIC
white, middle-class, female, straight, 17 yrs old, Gen 2020

GEOGRAPHIC
born here

PSYCHOGRAPHIC
Experiencer

BEHAVIORISTIC
strong worship attendance, whenever her youth group is active, attends worship in terms of previous

THEOLOGICAL
developing parents are moderate – progressive

ALYCE

DEMOGRAPHIC
female, white, middleclass, straight, widow, 77 yrs old, Boomer

GEOGRAPHIC
born here

PSYCHOGRAPHIC
Survivor

BEHAVIORISTIC
attends worship weekly, active in a range of church activities, officer in the church

THEOLOGICAL
conservative

TODD

DEMOGRAPHIC
male, celebrates Cherokee heritage, upper middle class, gay, 46 yrs old, Gen X

GEOGRAPHIC
Migrated from larger city in northeast

PSYCHOGRAPHIC
Achiever

BEHAVIORISTIC
attends worship occasionally, no other church activities

THEOLOGICAL
unknown

Figure 3.2

laddering technique can help preachers deepen their construct of the congregation in relation to particular sermons:

- While interpreting the text and considering its competing messages or emphases, preachers can ask: What do the people in the focus group need? What attributes of the text resonate with or challenge them most? What would they choose to focus upon? These questions function similar to the opening question in laddering: Why did you choose this product or service?
- When moving from what the ancient text "said" to what they want the contemporary sermon to "say," preachers can use the focus group to help sharpen the hermeneutical analogy. How does the situation of the text relate to the situation of the focus group's members' lives? How might the proposed sermonic message function for the hearers? These questions parallel the second laddering question in marketing: "Why is it good or bad . . . ?"
- As preachers think about sermonic imagery, they can test to see how different metaphors and stories would or would not appeal to different focus group members. In the course of using different imagery throughout the sermon, is there some imagery to which every member of the focus group would relate emotionally? Is there imagery that helps the members of the focus group experience the message as especially significant for them? Are there images that connect to their highest values? This step parallels the third and final laddering question discussed earlier: "Why is this important to you?"

Advertisers' use of market segmentation and focus groups expands preachers' tools for understanding their congregation and empathetically constructing what they need from a sermon. Tools such as these help the preacher avoid general messages delivered to a general audience and instead target their particular congregation with a particularly significant message drawn from a particular biblical text.

Let's imagine a preacher working on a sermon and use the three persons listed above as part of an empathetic focus group. The text for the sermon is Isaiah 65:17–25:

> For I am about to create new heavens
>   and a new earth;
> the former things shall not be remembered
>   or come to mind.
> But be glad and rejoice forever
>   in what I am creating;
> for I am about to create Jerusalem as a joy,
>   and its people as a delight.
> I will rejoice in Jerusalem,
>   and delight in my people;
> no more shall the sound of weeping be heard in it,
>   or the cry of distress.
> No more shall there be in it
>   an infant that lives but a few days,
>   or an old person who does not live out a lifetime;
> for one who dies at a hundred years will be considered a
>   youth,
>   and one who falls short of a hundred will be considered
>   accursed.
> They shall build houses and inhabit them;
>   they shall plant vineyards and eat their fruit.
> They shall not build and another inhabit;
>   they shall not plant and another eat;
> for like the days of a tree shall the days of my people be,
>   and my chosen shall long enjoy the work of their hands.
> They shall not labor in vain,
>   or bear children for calamity;
> for they shall be offspring blessed by the LORD—
>   and their descendants as well.
> Before they call I will answer,
>   while they are yet speaking I will hear.
> The wolf and the lamb shall feed together,
>   the lion shall eat straw like the ox;
>   but the serpent—its food shall be dust!
> They shall not hurt or destroy
>   on all my holy mountain, says the LORD.

This is Third Isaiah's eschatological vision of a postexilic world, specifically a new Jerusalem. After centuries of war and decades of exile in Babylon, the Persian king Cyrus allows exiled Jews to return home, rebuild the holy city and its temple, and have some level of self-rule. At its root, the oracle is an expression of hope that God's peace will become a reality in Judah and beyond.

Let's imagine our preacher wants to create a sermon that offers hearers the same kind of hope but decides that she must deal with the realities of contemporary violence and cynicism, such that hope for God's peace does not appear to be pie-in-the-sky, unrealistic wishmaking. How is she to approach this sermonic goal in relation to the varieties of hearers in her congregation?

First, she could ask the laddering question, "What attributes of the text resonate or challenge them most?," and come to name some specific ways the promise of peace seems unrealistic to the different members of the focus group. Drawing on demographic categories, at the two ends of the generations represented in the focus group, Alyce was born during World War II and has seen the United States engage in numerous wars, while Maggie was born after the attacks of September 11, 2001, and has never known an America not at war in Afghanistan. Todd makes known his pride in his Native American heritage, a people who have suffered greatly and experienced exile due to oppression and war waged by the U.S. government.

Moving up the ladder to the second set of questions, the preacher could inquire, "How does the situation of the text relate to the situation of the focus group members' lives? How might the proposed sermonic message function for the hearers?" In terms of behavioristic patterns of engagement with the church, only Alyce is likely to be biblically literate enough to know much about the exile and Isaiah. Yet from conversing with her in a weekly Bible study, the pastor knows that her theological tendency is to read Old Testament prophets as pointing to Jesus as the messiah. All three members of the imaginary focus group will need some introduction to Isaiah and the situation facing the prophet's original audience for them to connect emotionally with the message of this passage. A sermon on this text can function to draw the hearers into a sociotheological understanding of a prophetic worldview proffered by Scripture.

Moving to the final laddering question, the preacher would ask, "Is there some imagery to which every member of the focus group could relate emotionally? Is there imagery that helps the focus group members experience the message as especially significant for them?" In terms of psychographic segmentation, the preacher is addressing a young Experiencer who appears to be mainly concerned about fitting in with her peers, a middle-aged Achiever mainly focused on advancing his career, and an elderly Survivor who does not look much toward the future but instead often longs for the way things used to be. None of these are especially social justice–minded or concerned with issues of peace generally. The preacher knows she must first invite them to become emotionally connected with the need for peace and then invested in a realistic glimpse of what commitment to peace might look like.

The following sermon is an example of an attempt to use the above congregational segmentation and focus group observations to shape a message to address the particularities of a congregation. The opening of the sermon evokes the memory of a well-known nineteenth-century painting, an inexpensive print of which hangs in the church. Given that some might be unfamiliar with the painting, a copy is included on the front of the bulletin. The distance in time allows the hearers to see the painter's situation and slowly begin investing themselves existentially. The goal of the opening is to begin naming how unrealistic hope for peace seems. The specific mention of wars against Native Americans would especially be compelling to Todd.

> Edward Hicks couldn't earn a living as a Quaker minister back in the early 1800s, so he turned to painting. His most famous painting is the familiar *Peaceable Kingdom*. We have a print of *Peaceable Kingdom* hanging in our fellowship hall and a picture of that print is on the front of the worship bulletin.[29] Do

you know why the painting is so famous? It's famous because he painted sixty-two versions of that one scene. Sixty-two!

I don't believe Hicks could have painted all of those peaceable pictures if news back then worked the way it does now. He didn't have MSNBC, Fox News, and CNN on TV 24/7. He didn't have Google News notifications popping up every eighteen minutes. So he could sit in his studio in rural Pennsylvania and paint lambs and wolves eating together without thinking about all the fighting going on throughout his lifetime.

After all, this guy was born in the middle of the American Revolutionary War.

- During his lifetime from 1780 to 1849,
  * the United States fought at sea against France;
  * we fought alongside Sweden in two Barbary Wars;
  * we fought against Spain over who got Florida;
  * and we fought the War of 1812 against the British.
- All the while our new white government constantly fought against Native Americans whose land we invaded in:
  * the Chickamauga Wars,
  * the Northwest Indian War,
  * Tecumseh's War,
  * the Creek War,
  * two Seminole Wars,
  * the Texas-Indian Wars,
  * the Winnebago War,
  * the Black Hawk War,
  * the Cayuse War, and
  * the Apache Wars.

There's no way Edward Hicks could have been naïve enough to believe in such a vision if he had owned a television or a smartphone. The peaceable kingdom is an eschatological fantasy.

Having used Hicks to establish the idea that hope for peace is naïve, the sermon moves to the contemporary. Establishing an analogy between the nineteenth-century painter and today primes the hearers for the same sort of analogy to function between Isaiah and today later in the sermon. The list of contemporary wars begins with Afghanistan and a specific mention of youth in the church. The list moves from literal wars to other forms of violence and division (metaphorical wars, but situations literally lacking peace).

> I mean no one here, today, would be naïve enough to believe in a peaceable kingdom.
>
> • We have been at war in Afghanistan since 2001, longer than any member of our youth group has been alive.
> • Syria is a mess.
> • North Korea is working on nuclear missiles, and Iran has lost their economic incentives not to build nuclear weapons.
> • On our southern border, we are at war with people whose lives are so horrible that they walk a thousand miles in hope for a new home. We can have a healthy debate about immigration without calling these people drug dealers and rapists, taking their children away from them and putting them in cages, and forcing them to wait months for a hearing, all while we are reducing the number of lawyers and judges available to work with them.
> • There are on average forty violent homicides a day in this country.
> • In our Congress, partisanship has reached an all-time high.
> • The number of shootings of African Americans in recent years along with the rise of white supremacist hate speech recently led a civil rights activist I know to worry aloud that a race war might be coming.
>
> Peaceable kingdom? Don't make me laugh!
> Edward Hicks painted sixty-two beautiful pictures, but I can give ten thousand reasons why each one of them is naïve.

The end of the previous section invites the congregation to join the preacher in skepticism. They certainly know that the preacher will change directions soon, but the long list of current events is not about providing information. It is about creating a cumulative effect that begins to invite hearers to make an emotional connection with an overwhelming sense of violence and conflict in the world.

Having called Hick naïve and then with some distress naming why we cannot be naïve in that way today, the preacher takes the hearers back to Isaiah 65, which was read earlier in the service.

> I guess when Isaiah first cast that vision of a peaceable kingdom, the world was a kinder, gentler world. Our reading from Isaiah 65 offers a beautiful vision of a new Jerusalem, a new earth in which even different levels of the food chain will exist in harmony:
>
>> The wolf and the lamb shall feed together,
>>   the lion shall eat straw like the ox;
>>   but the serpent—its food shall be dust!
>> They shall not hurt or destroy
>>   on all my holy mountain, says the LORD.
>
> You might remember that the book of Isaiah is sixty-six chapters long, and its content actually stretches across a couple of hundred years. Scholars argue that the content comes from three different time periods. Our reading comes from the next to last chapter of the book. Even though you won't find it labeled this way in your Bibles, this section is commonly called Third Isaiah. Third Isaiah was written after the Persian Empire conquered the Babylonian Empire. It was the Babylonian Empire that had conquered Judah, destroyed the Jerusalem Temple, and taken much of Judah's population into exile. King Cyrus was determined to rule his lands more justly than his Babylonian predecessors, and thus he allowed the exiled peoples to return home and have some level of self-rule. Some parts of Third Isaiah even refer to Cyrus as a messiah.
>
> The prophecy recorded in Isaiah 65 is about this postexilic period when those who chose to return from exile were joined with those who had been left behind, and they joined together to rebuild the temple, to rebuild Jerusalem. Isaiah 65

envisions a new day of peace in the Middle East in the sixth century BCE. The language of the wolf and the lamb feeding together is a metaphor of hope that countries back then and over there like Babylon and Persia and Judah could finally coexist in harmony. Things were good, so Isaiah didn't have to deal with the kinds of divisions and fighting and killing we see today. The prophet could afford to cast such a vision in such a day of peace, but that doesn't do us any good. Our world doesn't look as promising at the moment. Peaceable kingdom? Don't make me laugh!

But did you know that Edward Hicks's paintings of the peaceable kingdom aren't really based on our reading today from Isaiah 65? They're based on Isaiah 11:

> The wolf shall live with the lamb,
>   the leopard shall lie down with the kid,
> the calf and the lion and the fatling together,
>   and a little child shall lead them.
> The cow and the bear shall graze,
>   their young shall lie down together;
>   and the lion shall eat straw like the ox.

And actually, Isaiah 65 is also based on Isaiah 11. Hear that? Isaiah 65 draws its imagery from Isaiah 11. Do you get why that changes everything? Third Isaiah takes its hope for a peaceable kingdom from First Isaiah!

First Isaiah was written some two hundred years earlier in a time when justice was fleeting, the oppressed needed rescuing, the orphan needed aid, and the widow needed defending (1:16–17).

- First Isaiah lives in a time when he sees Judah as spiraling into idolatry and humiliation.
- First Isaiah indicts the upper classes for their treatment of the less economically fortunate.
- First Isaiah is concerned about Jerusalem being attacked by Israel and Aram . . . and Assyria isn't far behind . . . and Babylon will follow Assyria! War after war after war on the horizon.

There is no accusing First Isaiah of naiveté. The vision he casts and that Third Isaiah *recasts* is one of hope in the midst of all the violence and hatred and oppression the world can muster. It is no escapist fantasy of utopia from someone out lying in a field of dandelions gazing at the clouds. First Isaiah knew the very real threat of the wolves and lions and serpents cast in the clothing of kings and generals and the privileged. I am amazed at the faith and hope for peace and reconciliation that is so often found in people who are anything but naïve.

Having established a connection with First Isaiah and claimed that hope for peace *in the midst* of conflict is not to be scoffed at as naïve but to be honored as true faith, the sermon turns to honor such hope in today's world of conflict. It does so by telling a story of a retired college professor. His age and life experiences are intended to resonate with Alyce. The fact that he is in a college setting connects with Maggie's thinking about the next phase of her life after high school. And his concern about racial justice will connect with Todd, since the issue of racial violence against Native Americans has already been raised and is mentioned here again explicitly. The emotional connections will hopefully lead hearers to identify with the main character of the story and to claim his values as their own.

Russell Compton was in his eighties when I first came to know him. A retired religion and philosophy professor and a retired United Methodist minister, he was born in 1909.

- For the first nine years of his life, the U.S. was engaged in the Border War with Mexico.
- When he was five, World War I broke out.
- When he was fourteen, the Last Indian Uprising was subdued.
- When he was thirty, World War II began to be waged across Europe and the U.S. joined in, following Pearl Harbor, when he was thirty-two.
- When he was forty-one, the Korean War.
- When he was fifty-two, the Vietnam War.

- When he was seventy-four, the U.S. invaded Granada.
- When he was eighty-one, the Gulf War.

No one could call Russell naïve. Yet in spite of all the war he had seen he was an outspoken pacifist. He worked his whole life to bring about peace in different forms.

As a young professor at Hendrix College, he brought a Black civil rights activist to campus in the 1950s to speak to his white students. The next year he was looking for a job.

As an older professor in the 1960s and '70s in Indiana, he helped students make their way to Canada or into the ministry to avoid dying in a war he considered unjust. As a retired professor, he visited the federal prison every week to offer prisoners grace and to condemn a system of incarceration that was racist.

In spite of all this, he always thought himself a failure as someone on the side of social justice because he had never been arrested during a protest.

Russell had been retired for almost 25 years, but he continued being active on campus as a volunteer chaplain, and the school dedicated a Peace and Justice Center in his honor.

The student-run radio station decided to interview the Grand Wizard of Indiana's Ku Klux Klan. There was going to be a march, and one of the student talk shows wanted to expose him for his hatred. The university wouldn't allow the interview to occur unless someone from the university was on the panel to counter whatever he might say. But no faculty member was willing to give him voice, so everyone said no. No administrator would share the stage with him.

Ninety-year-old Russell said yes when the radio station called him. I couldn't believe it. He had given much of his life to the cause of racial justice. I pressed him not to. I argued that to debate the Grand Wizard would give his hatred some form of unintended credence. Do you not know how awful these people are, how much violence they intend? I reminded him that he took students to the March on Washington where they heard King give his "I Have a Dream" speech. I asked him,

"Are you really naïve enough to think you can change this man's mind?"

He answered, "I don't know whether I can change his mind or not. But I do know that if I refuse to engage him in dialogue, I absolutely can't change his mind. I believe in a God who changes things, who redeems the unredeemable. I'll talk with him. Who knows what might come of it?"

Peaceable Kingdom? Sometimes God makes me laugh.

4

Advertising and Sermonic Forms

In the previous chapter we proposed ways of drawing on advertising's market research—segmentation and focus groups—to help develop a message to address the particular variety of hearers in one's congregation. We turn now to advertising to learn ways to shape the unfolding of such a message across the length of a sermon in order to effectively communicate that message. What processes are involved to increase the chances for achieving the desired outcomes?

Concern with how a sermon unfolds—with its *sermonic form*—has been central to homiletics since the early 1970s. Before then, most preachers used two main forms. The first is the Puritan Plain Style sermon that begins with *exegesis* of a biblical text, followed by *interpretation* of the text in theological terms, and finally *application* of that interpretation to the specific congregation being addressed. The second traditional form is the three-point sermon, which need not be exactly three points. This approach is thematic. The preacher opens by presenting a theme for the sermon and then breaks it into different points or subthemes.[1]

In the 1970s, homileticians began to recognize that the communication situation was changing (see chapter 2). For example, traditional theological and biblical terminology in the church was considered to be worn out and vacant of contemporary meaning. Also, the cultural shift brought on by radio, then movies, and then television changed what engaged audiences and congregations. Fred B. Craddock made the simple but profound argument that preachers should shift from the deductive mode exemplified in the Puritan Plain Style and three-point sermons to an inductive approach—move from the particulars of experience toward a point at which listeners draw conclusions for themselves.[2] Eugene L. Lowry took Craddock's inductive flow and added to it a specific narrative logic or structure for sermons commonly known as the Lowry Loop.[3] Meanwhile Henry Mitchell presented African American preaching as a form of inductive preaching moving from the human condition to celebration rooted in God's sovereignty.[4] Later David Buttrick argued from a phenomenological perspective for preaching in sequential moves that creates a shared, communal consciousness.[5]

As time marched on, however, the situation facing the church continued to change. Instead of being concerned with traditional ecclesial language being overused, preachers recognized that such language was unknown by more and more listeners. And outside the church, the Internet was changing the ways people receive communication—in different ways than they had with television. Instead of arguing for a specific sermonic form, some homileticians argued that preachers need to use a variety of rhetorical structures for different messages, purposes, and contexts.[6]

How might advertising enter this conversation to help preachers think through the issue of choosing rhetorical structures that are effective in communicating God's good news?

FCB GRID

While using a range of approaches to develop advertisements and assess their effectiveness, advertisers primarily turn to two long-standing, well-known models. The first is the FCB Grid, which is named after the advertising agency at which Richard Vaughn developed it in 1980—Foote, Cone and Belding.[7] The FCB Grid[8] is a two-dimensional model that positions products in one of four quadrants based on a consumer's *level* of involvement (high or low) with the product and his/her *type* of involvement with the product (thinking or feeling).

	THINK	FEEL
HIGH INVOLVEMENT	I Informative (Learn-Feel-Do)	II Affective (Feel-Learn-Do)
LOW INVOLVEMENT	III Habitual (Do-Learn-Feel)	IV Satisfaction (Do-Feel-Learn)

Several modifications have been suggested over the years, but using the FCB Grid provides advertisers with messaging ideas based on the order of the process (e.g., learn-feel-do) as well as the type and level of intensity experienced by consumers in relation to a product or service. For example, consumers may first think about information concerning a brand (learn), form an attitude (feel), and then act—such as making a purchase (do). Each quadrant can alter in messaging strategy in order to be most effective in touching the consumers' reasons for purchasing and the relationship they have with the product.

Consumers in the market for a car, for example, would be found in the upper left or right quadrants, representing high involvement and either high thinking or high feeling. High-involvement product decisions are important to consumers and typically include monetary or social risk, or both, as well as require strong consideration by the consumer.[9] A person might buy a car for its functional use to get from A to B. Here the person is most likely using functional information to make the choice, is concerned about the monetary risk in the purchase, and will put time into making a decision about what car to purchase. Messaging for this consumer would be informative and fact-based.

In contrast, people buying a car who see a car as an extension of their identity will also be highly involved, but they will be more influenced by emotions and feelings related to ways they believe the car will offer a desired social benefit. Messaging for this type of consumer could provide facts about the car but would be more focused on self-esteem and ego benefits as well as associations with certain social groups. Advertising copy in this case could include something about a few key flashy features of the car but emphasize "how your friends will love the way you look."

Shifting to low-involvement decisions, these usually are not as important to the consumer as they come with minimal financial or social risk and thus require little consideration. Similar to high-involvement situations, though, a low-involvement decision can require some information and facts or can be based more on the experience of how the product makes the consumer feel. Because these are low-involvement decisions, however, the feelings are often invoked by habitual or satisfaction purchases. Low-involvement *habitual products* include items such as razors, detergent, or car fuel. Examples of *satisfaction products* are experiential in nature, such as beer, chewing gum, and greeting cards. Strategies for marketing habitual products might include loyalty programs to help people find simplicity and ease in purchasing the same brand without much thought, while knowing they are getting a discount or future free items. In the case of satisfaction products such as pizza, advertising strategies can focus on social factors and friends using the product in a feel-good experience.[10] Recognizing the different levels and types of involvement related to products helps advertisers shape ads that appeal to the appropriate level and type of involvement needed as well as move people into new quadrants to expand their relationship with the brand and the benefits they perceive.

Like advertisers, preachers know that sermons should address the intellectual, emotional, experiential, and behavioral interests and needs of their listeners. Preachers have long been taught that sermons need to have head, heart, and hands. Marvin A. McMickle, for example, draws on Aristotle's *logos*, *pathos*, and *ethos* to present these three dimensions of a good central message or purpose of a sermon.[11] The FCB Grid, however, can help preachers think about how different sermons need to emphasize different levels of cognitive, experiential, or behavioral elements to help the message be more effective. Sermons dealing with new or challenging theological concepts may need to focus more on intellectual aspects and be shaped to flow from learning to feeling then to doing. Those dealing with elements of Christian commitment and piety might lean more toward the experiential flow from sermonic imagery that creates feeling, which in turn leads to learning and finally doing. Sermons dealing with moral or ethical concerns and the Christian life might put more weight on the behavioral and begin with examples of doing that lead to learning and feeling.

Moreover, some homiletical topics may require different levels of involvement (intellectual or emotional) than others. For example, a topic that is familiar and comfortable to a congregation will not require much involvement to be effective. On the other hand, a topic that asks congregations to let go of unhealthy, unhelpful, or unorthodox elements of their worldview and replace them with new theological and existential claims may require a great deal more involvement. Such topics are rarely effective when offered in the course of a single sermon any more than a high-involvement purchase can be made on the spur of the moment. Preachers will need to address the topic carefully slowly across numerous sermons (see chapter 6).

AIDA

The second common approach advertisers use to develop advertising messages and assess an ad's effectiveness is known by the acronym *AIDA*, which stands for attention, interest, desire, and action. First, the advertiser must gain the *attention* of consumers so that they can be aware of a potential message.

Then the message must maintain the *interest* of consumers to generate the next step of having a *desire* to want the brand. Finally the advertiser must provide tangible *action* steps for consumers to undertake, such as purchasing the brand's products or visiting the company's website for more information.

A good example of AIDA in action is the well-known 2013 GEICO commercial using a real camel sauntering through a business office asking his coworkers to guess what day it is.[12] Viewers' *attention* is caught by the clash of a camel in a business office. No one in the office provides the answer, so the camel keeps pressing. The camel continues walking and engaging with the different office employees, repeatedly asking what day it is. The suspension of an answer along with the camel having a charismatic personification keeps the viewer *interested*. Finally, one woman in a reluctant and irritated tone replies, "Hump Day." The camel is delighted and yells out, "Hump Day!" A first-time viewer would have no idea what product is being advertised at this point but the humor would lead them to a *desire* to know. This whole scene serves as a set up for the punch line delivered by two musicians (also out of place in a business office) saying that customers who switch to GEICO insurance and save hundreds are "happier than a camel on Wednesday!" Finally, as the musicians begin playing, a voiceover states, "Get happy. Get GEICO. Fifteen minutes could save you 15 percent or more." The punch line relates to a common *action* promoted in GEICO ads during this time period: taking only fifteen minutes to apply for insurance on GEICO's website could save you as much as 15 percent on your premiums.

The ad was one of the most successful ads for GEICO in creating awareness of the brand, with 6.1 million views. In fact, 2019 marked the twenty-fifth anniversary between GEICO and the Martin Agency, creator of the Hump Day ad. To celebrate and garner publicity, consumers were allowed to vote on their all-time favorite GEICO ads out of eight classics selected. Hump Day from 2013 was the winner.[13] Also, the advertisement experienced 1.6 million online shares, of which 67.3 percent of sharing took place on Wednesdays.[14] This is a great example of understanding your audience and providing something to engage them enough that they want to share it with friends. In terms of market share, through its unique and quirky advertising, GEICO became the second-largest provider in the auto insurance market in 2013, beating Allstate.[15]

Let's examine each step of AIDA in more detail.

Attention

Before an ad can make its pitch for consumers to take a specific action (which is the whole purpose of an ad), it must first grab their attention. This is difficult given that there is so much noise in the communication setting in the sense of others also trying to grab a consumer's attention. Consumers are used to fast-forwarding through television ads, flipping past magazine ads, and hitting the close button on Internet ads (see chapter 1). Therefore, to grab attention, advertisers try creative and unexpected methods (like putting a camel in an office building). *Disruption* is the primary technique advertisers use. Disruption has many forms, taking the path of being unexpected, novel, or surprising—something with stopping power to break through all of the other sources vying for a consumer's attention.

Depending on the medium of the ad, disruption techniques for grabbing attention can involve the use of unusually bright colors or loud sounds, interesting or provocative imagery, humor, and a mixture of visual and linguistic elements to build a synergy of impact. A magazine ad for Diet Pepsi, for example, once grabbed attention with the provocative headline, "This year, hit the beach topless." The humorous visual underneath was of a cap from a Diet Pepsi bottle lying in the sand.[16]

Using a *headline* in an ad is also effective for causing disruption and capturing attention. The opening line can ask a question or make a controversial statement that generates curiosity or creates ambiguity. As David Ogilvy, often labeled the father of advertising, is famously quoted as stating, "The headline is the 'ticket on the meat.' Advertisers use it to flag down readers who are prospects for the kind of product you are advertising." Ogilvy is also quoted as saying, "On average five times as many people read the headlines as read the body copy."[17] Both of these ideas stress the importance of using smart and engaging headlines to stop your audience in order to gain their attention and awareness for your message. Imagine a toothpaste ad where the headline reads or the commercial opens with "People really like yellow and stained teeth." This statement immediately catches the audience's attention because it is the opposite of what consumers know to be true. Hopefully, people would be curious enough to read the body copy or watch the remainder of the commercial.

Ads that are *personalized* to the specific target audience's needs and desires can also be a form of disruption, as you are grabbing the attention of the listeners by the novelty of the message being personally relevant. This last point is similar to being in a crowded room with many people talking when you suddenly become aware someone has said your name. This technique is even more practical and possible today with Internet advertising, where ads are chosen for people based on their past search history, online purchases, and the like. It is disruptive to see an ad pop up on Facebook related to products you recently searched on Amazon.

Interest

Once advertisers have disrupted people to gain their attention, they have to keep and deepen their interest. Interest is maintained by creating *stickiness*, the mental engagement with a message. One measure for assessing the effectiveness of the content for websites promoting brands, for example, is the time a person spends on the website. How long do consumers stick on the site? Stickiness stems from developing messages that are *entertaining, memorable*, or *funny* but that are also personally relevant to the audience. Consider the provocative Diet Pepsi ad mentioned above. The headline "Hit the beach topless" quickly catches the readers' attention and invites women (who wear swimsuits with tops) to think about how their body looks in (or out of) a swimsuit. But then as readers look for the representation of a topless beach, they connect the cap-less Diet Pepsi and experience a momentary satisfaction with the connection and cleverness of the play on words as well as a desire to drink low-calorie soft drinks that will help them have the beach body they desire. This advertisement has put Diet Pepsi at the top of the readers' minds while doing it in a way that they feel rewarded and positive about the experience.

Developing messages that are entertaining, memorable, or funny are critically important to the stickiness of the message and the overall effectiveness of the advertisement but can create challenges. Entertaining messages keep the attention and interest of the audience, but entertainment is not the purpose of ads. It is just a means to an end. Entertaining images, storylines, and humor can obscure the main message if the advertiser is not careful about connecting these elements to the product in ways that are personally relevant to consumers. Everyone has experienced an ad that was entertaining and memorable, but they were unable later to recall the product being promoted. Similarly, all have watched a commercial that was intriguing and entertaining only to be confused about the connection between the content of the ad and the product promoted at the end. The most effective ads are those in which the entertaining, memorable, or humorous elements connect the viewer with the product in a provocative but explicit manner. In other words, the interest created in the ad leads to a desire related to the brand.

Desire

Once an advertisement grabs an audience's attention and deepens its interest, it must move to create desire for the brand by convincing consumers they need or want what the product offers. A *need* is some requirement or necessity of life a consumer seeks to fulfill—for example, food for providing energy to live. A *want*, on the other hand, is a benefit sought that is not necessary but is appealing for other reasons. A need for basic nutrition could be fulfilled by beans and rice or a salad, but a want for certain tastes might only be fulfilled by a steak, pizza, or candy. Advertisers learn what needs and wants consumers have by doing various types of market research, including segmentation and focus groups as discussed in the previous chapter.

As noted in the earlier discussion of the FCB Grid, most strategies used in advertising create desire by speaking to consumers' heads and hearts. In other words, advertisers try to present information and facts that consumers will find persuasive while also touching consumers' hearts and emotions to create appeal. Advertising approaches used to touch the head and heart (sometimes stressing one over the other) vary by product type, consumer segment, goals of the advertisers, and so on.

Demonstration, for example, is used when consumers have a problem that the brand will fix. Because many other products also exist that will fix the problem, advertisers add heart to the demonstration. Take as an example a commercial for Mr. Clean Magic Eraser Extra Durable.[18] The product is a cleaning pad that will "erase" stains on various surfaces. The thirty-second commercial opens with a view of crayon markings on a wall (not a picture—just scribbles, implying they were made by a very young child) with a side panel showing the words, "Mr. Clean vs. Crayon." Then the advertisement demonstrates how to use the pad and its effectiveness with three steps listed in the side panel while viewers see hands manipulating the cleaning pad and removing the crayon marking easily. The three steps are

1. Grab a Magic Eraser;
2. Wet, then squeeze out excess water;
3. Erase.

Finally, Mr. Clean is declared the winner over the crayon markings. All of this is done without any voiceover narration, which is unnecessary since the procedure is so simple. In fact, that seems to be the point of the demonstration. The effectiveness seen on screen is intended to create desire in the consumer. But what adds stickiness to the desire is the music playing during the commercial. It is a simple but catchy children's tune with the kind of instrumental arrangement one expects of music aimed at preschoolers. Without saying anything, the music evokes the innocence and playfulness of children that will result in things like scribbling on the wall. No need to be upset; just get Magic Eraser. The ad primarily makes an intellectual appeal and is personally relevant to viewers with small children, but the music adds heart.

More often than not, however, desire is created primarily by a *psychological appeal* rather than a rational one, connecting with consumers emotionally or experientially.

Different emotional valences across the spectrum of negative (unpleasant) to positive (pleasant) affectivity can be effective in advertising. For example, fear can create desire, as seen in ads selling a home alarm system where a house without an alarm is robbed or ads encouraging people not to drink and drive with a visual of a car accident showing what could happen if one does. One effective magazine ad shows a morgue with a corpse covered on a slab and only feet sticking out from underneath. On one foot is a toe tag with a design similar to a well-known cigarette brand and the words "Smoking kills."[19]

There are, of course, also happy and good-feeling psychological appeals in advertising. Soft-drink companies want people to connect feeling happy with their products so that consumers desire and purchase more. Coke ads have been especially effective with this approach from their iconic 1971 "I'd Like to Teach the World to Sing" ad [20] to their 2009 ad campaign, "Open Happiness."[21] The purpose of the product (in terms of needs and wants), combined with knowledge of consumers (as learned from market research described in the previous chapter), help advertisers determine what emotional valence works best in an ad. According to Frenay, happiness is the most used emotion in advertisements, and research indicates positive valence ads create pleasant associations in our brains that are easier to remember for longer periods of time. The emotion makes people feel good, often using images of family bonding, playfulness, romance, and adventure.[22]

Psychological appeals involve more than valence, however. Advertisers must also consider the intensity of arousal they want to create in consumers. To aim too high in a single ad will likely result in missing the mark. To aim too low will not create enough desire to lead consumers to act. Moderate arousal is a reasonable goal for an ad and has the potential to stick and be memorable.[23]

Some of the most popular and effective commercial formats for creating desire using psychological appeals are slice-of-life ads involving storytelling. These types of ads fit well with Millennials who seek products to create and change their identities. For advertisers, these techniques allow more than the functional benefits of the product to be highlighted and provide an outlet to show context of use and personalities associated with the brand image. Take, for example, the "Tribute to Moms" ad campaign developed by Procter and Gamble (P&G) over the past several Olympics. The typical commercial is about two minutes in length using a montage of images creating a mini drama showing how tough it is to be a mom while showing the support mothers provide their children who want to grow up to become world-class athletes.[24] As children grow from elementary-age to Olympic-age athletes, we see different mothers doing two different sets of tasks: everyday household work for their families (using P&G products) and attending athletic events where they rejoice and cry with their children's victories and defeats. Near the end of the commercial, text on the screen reads, "The hardest job in the world is the best job in the world. Thank you, Mom." Then in the last few seconds, as pictures of P&G products flash on screen, a woman's voice says, "P&G: Proud sponsor of moms." Viewers who love the Olympics and love the backstories of the various athletes competing cannot help but have a tear in their eye as the story of the ad unfolds through the different heartaches until the triumphant win at the Olympics in the end leaves a positive feeling about P&G that just brought you this wonderful mini drama. Mothers especially feel an emotional connection because their struggles and the importance of their roles have been honored.

Action

The final step with AIDA is the call to action. By the time an effective ad invites action, the consumer has been made aware of the brand's message, has become interested in it, and has felt a desire for it. Now the audience is ready to be given methods to act. In the action phase of an ad, the advertiser offers consumers incentives to act, hoping that they will lead to a purchase or related desired behavior, such as visiting a website or store for more information. Car companies often encourage coming to the dealership for a test drive and a free gift.

Infomercials are information-styled commercials providing detailed brand information that can be anywhere from a few minutes in length to as long as an hour. The traditional three-minute infomercial is strong at getting the attention and interest of the consumer while building desire for the brand. They make the need for the product personally relevant and so attractive that consumers feel compelled to act, even asking themselves how they have lived without this product in the past. One of the best-known ad campaigns at getting consumers to act was the series of Ginsu knives infomercials.[25] In the Ginsu infomercial, *attention* was grabbed with the disruption of a knife cutting a soda can and then still being able to cut through a tomato. *Interest* was deepened by showing how versatile the knife is at cutting different objects and foods and how the blade never dulls. The whole set of knives being offered, however, was not presented all at once. "But wait, there's more!" The number of knives offered kept expanding across the commercial with additional offerings thrown in such as a vegetable decorator. By the end of the ad, there were about ten knives, plus a vegetable decorating tool, and all for the irresistible low price of $9.95. *Desire* has been built slowly. To spur desire into *action*, viewers were told they could get this amazing product at this amazing price, but "Only if you call right now."

AIDA AND SERMON FORM

Preachers would do well to learn from advertisers and shape sermons to grab attention, deepen interest, create desire, and call for action, although some adaptation may be required since preaching's purposes are different than those of advertising. Before we explore using AIDA as a way to structure a sermon, it is important to acknowledge that there are well-known homiletical analogs to AIDA with which readers may already be familiar.[26]

First, there is the classic African American sermon form described as, "Start low, go slow, rise high, strike fire, and sit down."[27] When preachers start low and go slow they are exploring some element of the human condition, some bad news that needs addressing. Starting low and quiet grabs attention. Going slow and drawing out discussion of the bad news deepens interest and leads to a desire for good news in response. Good news begins when the preacher turns to rise high, and emotional arousal of the congregation rises high as well, until fire is struck and the preacher might call for action.

Second, Eugene L. Lowry proposes a homiletical form that is also very close to AIDA.[28] The Lowry Loop is a narrative structure/logic in which the preacher moves the listeners through five stages:

- Oops! Upset the equilibrium
- Ugh! Analyze discrepancy
- Aha! Clue to the resolution
- Whee! Experience of the gospel
- Yeah! Anticipate consequences

In relation to AIDA, *upsetting the equilibrium* felt by the hearers is equivalent to causing a disruption in order to grab attention. *Analyzing the discrepancy* now experienced deepens the interest in the hearers. Being given a *clue to the resolution* of the discrepancy creates a desire for that resolution. *Experiencing the good news* then leads to *anticipating consequences* that may include a need for action.

Comparison of AIDA with the classic African American form and Lowry Loop has suggested a point of required adaptation. In both comparisons, the parallelism is tenuous at the point of calling for action. While attention, interest, and desire clearly fit with the two homiletical approaches, a call for action does not fit with preaching as well.

"Preachy" in common idiom has a negative connotation implying one person telling others what to do (usually from a vantage point of self-righteousness). "Preaching," however, in its purest form does not include exhortation—self-righteous or otherwise. To preach is to offer good *news*. News is declarative in tone, not imperative. Thus, most sermons should not call people to act but instead should declare ways that God has acted and is acting on our behalf.[29] The pulpit is heir to the psychologizing of pastoral care, self-help movements in our culture, an ideology that values doing over speaking, the fallacy that one controls one's own fate, works righteousness, and so on. All of this homiletical inculturation makes it harder for preachers to say "is" than "should." But the good news of a sovereign God, a redeeming Christ, and an empowering Spirit calls for just that from faithful preachers. After all, when hearers are told, "You should," what they experience is the flip side of imperative: accusation. The "should" implies a condemnation of the hearers for ways they have not already been living up to the command of the sermon. Instead of creating desire to act, the hortatory sermon creates guilt for past inaction.

The exception to this restriction, of course, is when the biblical text upon which a sermon is based is itself hortatory material. If the original author, narrator, or speaker behind or in a passage tells others what to do, it might be appropriate for the preacher to take an analogous stance with a contemporary congregation. In truth, however, preachers apply a message taken from a biblical passage to a congregation by telling them something they can or should do much more often than biblical texts invite. Therefore, we approach AIDA with "action" referring to God's work instead of ours as a standard approach, but recognizing that at times preachers need to call congregations to act ethically in response to and in concert with God's action.

To return to a metaphor from Eugene Lowry, every sermon needs to move from an itch to a scratch. Hearers need to be made itchy about the existential issue at hand so that they want and are ready to receive relief brought when the good news scratches the itch. The movement from establishing the itch to offering the scratch must flow smoothly so as to bring hearers to a point of investment in that scratch. Structuring a sermon using AIDA can do this. Let's turn to a sermon structured in this way to illustrate the form's effectiveness.

The following sermon was preached by O. Wesley Allen, Jr. at a graduation worship service at Perkins School of Theology, Southern Methodist University, on May 17, 2019. The service came at the end of a semester in which a special session of the General Conference of the United Methodist Church had voted for a "Traditional Plan" that continued past practices of excluding gay persons from being ordained and prohibiting same-sex marriages from being performed in a United Methodist church or by a United Methodist clergyperson while adding punitive measures for clergy who broke these rules. Much of the talk around the school for months had involved the divisiveness of the denomination and the uncertainty about graduates' place in the future of the denomination. This situation, in part, led student planners to choose "Worship, Diversity, Unity" as the theme for the service. The passage chosen for the sermon was 1 Corinthians 14:26–33a:

> What should be done then, my friends? When you come together, each one has a hymn, a lesson, a revelation, a tongue, or an interpretation. Let all things be done for

building up. If anyone speaks in a tongue, let there be only two or at most three, and each in turn; and let one interpret. But if there is no one to interpret, let them be silent in church and speak to themselves and to God. Let two or three prophets speak, and let the others weigh what is said. If a revelation is made to someone else sitting nearby, let the first person be silent. For you can all prophesy one by one, so that all may learn and all be encouraged. And the spirits of prophets are subject to the prophets, for God is a God not of disorder but of peace.

Attention

In the worship bulletin, the sermon title was listed as "There's a Bomb in the Steeple." The provocative title helps grab the congregation's attention before the preacher ever steps into the pulpit. But attention is especially caught when in the opening lines of the sermon the preacher radically and surprisingly shifts tone from pleasantries to strong (albeit playful) language challenging the choice of the theme for the service. The headline sort of language is intentionally disruptive and abrupt.

> Congratulations. Graduation is an important rite of passage in which you move from ministry while you are in school to ministry as someone who wishes they were back in school, when you move from splitting your energy between studying and the little bit of time we leave for anything else to splitting your time between deleting Perkins emails asking you for money and the little bit of time we leave for anything else.
>
> I want to thank you for inviting me to preach to you and your families and friends on this special day. It is an honor to stand before you.
>
> That said, What the hell?! The theme for the service is "Worship, Diversity, Unity"?! Just like a bunch of naive seminary students to pick a theme that ties diversity and unity together with worship in today's climate.

Interest

Following the attention-grabbing hook, the preacher does not let up. He challenges whether unity is a realistic expectation in the current state of affairs. Interest in this question, this itch, is deepened by beginning with the division in the United Methodist Church, moving to the wider church, and then moving out to culture. At the key point in this deepening movement, the preacher tells a story from which the title of the sermon is drawn, making clear that the bomb in the steeple is a metaphor for how explosive division in the church is. The metaphor sets up an interpretation of the situation of conflict which Paul is addressing in his letter and Paul's call for unity rooted in love and for the purpose of building up the church.

> Have you not been paying attention? The United Methodist Church is falling apart. Etymologically "diversity" and "division" share the same root: divide. There is little room there for unity, much less worshiping in unity, when the church is so divided. *It is ugly and likely to get uglier.*
>
> While what's happening in the United Methodist Church is especially raw for some of us, let's be clear: The United Methodists have no monopoly on conflict. We are in an age of congregations and denominations fighting, dividing. Communities going different directions. Individuals just leaving.
>
> But it's not just in the church. We are a divided culture with a divisive government. The president may be the master at incendiary tweets, but others on both sides of the aisle are catching up quickly. Civility in political debate, if there ever was such a thing, is certainly gone now. And here we are starting a new election cycle with 428 Democrats running for president. It's hard to imagine, but this election cycle might be uglier than last time.
>
> There's a nonprofit agency I know that has had poor management for more than a decade. A new executive director was hired to clean things up, but the staff is resistant to any changes. They keep saying, "We've never done it that way

before." That's not just a church saying. They have raised the conflict to such a level that the institution may have to close because it can't move forward. See, that's not just a church thing either. *It's ugly.*

Division is everywhere. But I guess it is especially painful, especially disillusioning, when it's in the church. Especially since it seems to permeate every aspect of church life far beyond deep ethical issues like the inclusion of homosexuals in the rites and life of the church. Organ music versus guitar and drums. Should our limited funds go to the youth program, to worship, to disaster relief . . . or to polishing the fellowship hall floor? (We, of course, know the floor is going to win.) There's bickering about the staff. Bickering among the staff. I hear from students of fistfights by elderly women in the choir. (Don't you mess with the altos!) The conflict and division in the church is ugly. And it's tiring. And it's painful.

You remember the metaphor, don't you, where the church is compared to Noah's Ark? The saying goes, "If it weren't for the rain outside, you couldn't stand the stench inside."

An author tells of visiting a Croatian village that had been bombed extensively in the horrific ethnic conflicts of the Bosnian War in the 1990s. In the village there was a church with an unexploded bomb lodged in the steeple. The author was amazed that the people continued worshiping in the building with that bomb ready to go off any moment right overhead.[30] When I read the article about that church, my first thought was, "How horrible!" But then my second thought was, "Heck, every church I've ever known was filled with bombs waiting to explode overhead in the steeple. Every church I've ever served had land mines hidden around in the basement."

Conflict and division are all around us in the church. It's terribly ugly. But it's not new. It's pretty much as old as the church itself.

In fact, one of the earliest writings of the New Testament is basically a case study for church conflict that is about as ugly as it can get: First Corinthians. The cluster of house churches in Corinth had become divided between the right and the left, between the strong and the weak, between the poor and the rich.

- They were divided over baptism.
- They were divided at the table.
- They were divided around their favorite preachers.
- They were divided over whether to marry.
- They were divided about eating meat.
- They were divided over resurrection and eschatology.
- They were so divided some ended up in civil court.

And you thought we were special. Nope, no new conflict under the sun.

In the passage we read, Paul is prescribing an approach for orderly worship. But as you know, that passage is really at the tail end of a longer section of the letter dealing with division over spiritual gifts. A big section. Almost 20 percent of the letter is dedicated to this one issue. The church is arguing about what spiritual gift is the most important gift for Christians to have. They're fussing about whether you can even say you have a spiritual gift if you don't speak in tongues. They're shouting in the pews:

We've got the Spirit, yes we do.
We speak in tongues, how 'bout you?!

Paul begins addressing this issue by affirming everyone's different gifts and showing how important they all are for the church. They all come from the same Spirit, and in their diversity they work together to serve the one Body of Christ. I describe the church as Noah's Ark and bombs waiting to explode overhead, but Paul takes the high road and says, "Body of Christ." That's why he was an apostle and I am not.

Anyway, after this, the apostle moves to love. While we all have lots of different gifts, he says, we all share one gift—the foundational spiritual gift from which all other gifts arise—love. You can speak in tongues, you can be a great preacher, you can give away everything you own to the poor, but if you don't have love, all of it means nothing. Love is the greatest spiritual gift, Paul says. Even greater than faith or hope.

Still, in the love chapter that is so misused in weddings every day of the year, Paul deconstructs all the claims about who has the greater gift when he says everyone has the greatest gift. He brings everyone together with the greatest common denominator: all we need is love.

Now Paul is ready to address the issue of speaking in tongues and prophecy. Paul addresses them using the groundwork he laid concerning the diversity of spiritual gifts and the unity of love. All spiritual gifts, he says, should be measured as to how well they build up the church instead of whether they build up the persons who possess the gifts.

Let me see if I can connect that to technical seminary lingo you have heard while studying at Perkins. I think, the proper theological phrase in the original Latin is, "It's not about you." In English that translates to, "It's not about you." Spiritual gifts and vocation in the church ... are about the church.

So when speaking in tongues in the Corinthian house churches lifts up others in the church, especially through interpretation, they all have a purpose. When they lift up the person speaking in tongues, Paul says, the church has no need of it. Whatever spiritual gift you have to add into the mix of the wide diversity of gifts in the church is measured by the standard of love.

That applies as well, says Paul, to worship. And finally we return to the short passage we read a few minutes ago. You thought I'd forgotten about the passage, but I got us back around to it. Paul is calling for order in worship not because he is obsessive compulsive, not because he has taken Introduction to Worship and knows the fourfold ordo. No, he calls for order so that each gift might used according to love:

When you come together,
    each one has a hymn,
    a lesson,
    a revelation,
    a tongue,
    or an interpretation.

Let all things be done for building up.

Unity of purpose of building up the church shaped by love in the midst of diversity of gifts equals true worship. Paul's ethic of love aimed at bringing unity and upbuilding to worship in the midst of the amazing diversity of spiritual gifts in the church has been a gift to the church throughout its history.

Desire

Having intensified the sense of conflict that is facing graduates in their coming ministries and named Paul's response to such conflict in his day, the next movement of the sermon creates a desire in hearers to experience the unifying love in the midst of diversity Paul talks about in contemporary terms. This preacher does this by telling a story about a pastor of the church in which he was raised.

I was raised in Sylacauga, Alabama. *Sylacauga* is a Cherokee word that means "buzzard roost" and never was a town better named. Take all of the stereotypes you have of a small town in Alabama, inject those stereotypes with steroids, and you've got Sylacauga in the sixties and seventies when I was a mere babe.

My family attended First United Methodist Church in Sylacauga. That church loved me into the faith.

The Reverend Daniel C. Whitsett had been pastor at Sylacauga First Church before I was born. Well, when he was there it was First Methodist Church, because the merger with the Evangelical United Brethren Church hadn't made us "United" yet.

Dan came to the church as a young minister not long out of seminary. It was in the late forties, just after World War II. Although a small town, Sylacauga had grown during the war because a munitions factory had been built there. I imagine they built bombs that were the forebears of the one found in the steeple in Croatia.

First Methodist Church was a stepping-stone for Dan on his way to become bishop. The church hierarchy had slated him for the episcopacy early on because he had all the marks of Methodist success about him, all the right spiritual gifts to help him go places.

One of those marks was love. Rev. Whitsett visited people in their homes so much that no one was sure if he ever lived in the parsonage. He talked with youth instead of just preaching at them. He started the preschool and kindergarten at the church that is still there today because he loved children. In that church, he baptized babies, confirmed adolescents, married young adults, and buried the elderly. He was especially known for the love he showed when people were sick. If someone was in the hospital, he got there before the doctor. He loved the people of First Church Sylacauga, and they loved him.

Dan came to the church in the late forties but stayed into the mid-fifties. While he was at First Church, the decision in *Brown v. Board of Education* was announced in 1954, exactly sixty-five years ago today. Of course, it would be nearly ten years before that decision was implemented in Alabama and the public schools were integrated. But Dan Whitsett began right away preaching that the church should support integration, and that Christians should view all of God's children as equal.

He used what he learned in seminary; he used his spiritual gifts in Scripture, theology, ethics, sociology, and psychology to argue for this justice issue. So in the mid-fifties, when most white pulpits in Alabama heard a domesticated, individualistic, and too-often racist distortion of the gospel, First Methodist Church in Sylacauga heard God calling them into the reign of God in a radically new way. In worship, they were built up to overcome the divisions in society between whites and Blacks.

The Ku Klux Klan began riding around the outside of the church honking their horns during the worship hour. Racist graffiti was painted on the church doors more than once. And a cross was burned in the front yard of the parsonage.

Some church members left, but most people stayed and supported Rev. Whitsett. I suspect to some degree they sat in the pews with their arms folded and cotton balls in their ears, but they stayed. They stayed and tolerated Dan because he loved them before he prophesied to them.

Action

Desire for finding love in the church to be unifying in the midst of diversity is created in the previous movement but not fully satisfied. Rev. Whitsett's story is compelling, but the final paragraph leaves some satisfaction yet to be found. His love kept people in the church in spite of bigotry, but there is no evidence that real change in the hearts and minds of the congregation occurred. The final movement of the story finishes Rev. Whitsett's story of combating racism by connecting it with the preacher's own early ministry in which he faced racism in the church. The conclusion declares God's unifying and loving action without removing the bomb from the steeple. The tension between God's just and loving action in the past and continued conflict in the church over race offer realistic hope for graduates heading out into ministry instead of a sentimental utopian picture of the church.

It is worth noting that while the sermon explicitly names God's action and does not call hearers to act, the model of ministry of Rev. Whitsett is implicitly offered for hearers as a way of being and acting in their own ministry. This element is appropriately offered since Paul speaks in the imperative in the section read from 1 Corinthians. Nevertheless, the imperative tone is kept at the implicit level to be more inviting.

As you know, Paul wrote at least four letters to the Corinthian churches. The letter we call First Corinthians was actually his second one, but no one preserved the real first one. The letter we call Second Corinthians was likely his fourth letter but may contain fragments of the third one in it. I'm only mentioning this so I can build up a little street cred with the New Testament faculty.

But now that I've mentioned it anyway, I guess I should note that the eloquence of Paul's argument about unity and diversity in First Corinthians didn't seem to work to quell the Corinthian conflict. By the time we get to Paul's fourth letter, the divisions in the church had risen to the level that Paul is having to defend his apostleship.

Of course, we don't know what happens later. Maybe long after Paul was out of the picture, conflict won the day. But maybe Paul's plea for love as the reigning ethic won the day. I mean, you never know what God will do in the future when someone brings the spiritual gift of love to bear on conflict in the present.

Like Paul's ministry in Corinth, Dan Whitsett's ministry didn't end with his picture on a poster for success in conflict management. He loved the people of Sylacauga First Church and tried to lead them through one of the great divisions of our history—white oppression of African Americans. But as it goes with all Methodist pastors, the time came for Dan to move on.

The problem was that no other church in Alabama would have him in 1958. His proclamation of the social gospel in relation to the sin of racism cost him greatly, so much that he would never be able to be elected bishop. In fact, he would never serve in Alabama again. He was sent to a church in Cambridge, Massachusetts. [PAUSE]

I started serving my first church, also in Alabama, at the age of nineteen when I was a college student. It was the mid-1980s. God bless that poor twenty-two-member church that loved me into the ministry even while listening to the worst sermons ever preached on the face of this planet.

But I thought about Dan some there because I faced racism in the church within months of having arrived. We were so small the church didn't have even a handful of children—after all the average age of church members was 603. I wanted to start a summer children's program with community kids.

The church loved the idea, so long as I didn't include the African American kids from the community. I almost left the ministry over that. Thirty years after Dan Whitsett had fought against segregation in the school system and here I was still facing it in the so-called body of Christ. It was ugly.

I think the main thing that kept me in the ministry and kept me at that church was that part of my trying to learn how to be a better pastor there had involved going down into the basement underneath the sanctuary and reading through decades worth of Board minutes so I would know the church's history and ethos.

In those minutes I found a petition that had circulated around all Alabama Methodist churches in 1967 concerning the upcoming merger of the Methodist Church with the Evangelical United Brethren. The hot-button issue was that the EUB Church was requiring the Methodist Church to discontinue its practice of segregating white and Black churches for the merger to happen. The petition stated that if the merger took place, the churches that had signed off on it would pull out of the denomination.

As I looked down the list of churches on that wicked piece of paper, I saw that every Methodist church in the Sylacauga District had signed ... every church except one ... every church except the one that Dan Whitsett had pastored in the time of segregation and that had later loved me into the faith.

So I stayed in the ministry, and I stayed at that church. Because you really never know what God will do in the future when someone brings the spiritual gift of love to bear on conflict in the present.

5

Sermonic Imagery and Narrative Advertising

The advertising formula of attention, interest, desire, and action (AIDA) that we discussed in the previous chapter is a model that helps move the consumer through the different stages of a message to the desired actionable outcome. In today's world those stages of an ad often need to include more than simply informing the consumer about a product or service. They need to create an experience for consumers that will lead them to act. One of the techniques advertisers have used to garner attention, increase interest, and deepen desire is storytelling.

THE POWER OF NARRATIVE STICKINESS

Narrative advertising has grown significantly in recent years and will continue to grow as brands shift more and more from traditional information-based advertising to being generators of content by collaborating with networks and media companies.

In large part, this new direction has been forced on advertisers as the shift in technology has changed the power relationship between advertisers and consumers. As presented in chapter 1, consumers today are more in control than ever of the advertising with which they interact—they can skip advertising at the press of a button on a remote control or with the click of a mouse. Advertisers must provide stories that consumers want to tune into and engage. As one writer for *Adweek*, a leading advertising industry publication, states, "The golden age of advertising may be coming to a close, but the golden age of storytelling is just getting started. Don't skip it."[1]

Everyone likes a good story because humans are "wired for stories."[2] People are willing to give of their time to be entertained if the story is interesting and personally engaging. Research on narrative advertising and storytelling discusses the many benefits of this technique.[3] Stories exist and are valued across all cultures, age groups, languages, and religions. They are able to communicate information that is emotionally charged and relatable, which in turn makes that information memorable. Because they are part of our regular communication, stories provide a framework for new knowledge that is easily processed. Storytelling can also be used to help audiences see connections, context, and relationships in new ways.[4] Storytelling allows for the storyteller to set up a simulation of the experience where the audience's minds and imaginations take on the role of the protagonist and they are actively engaged in the elements of the story as the speaker unfolds them.[5]

To show the power of story in advertising over instructional kinds of ads, let's compare two ways of advertising emergency room (ER) services.[6] Imagine an ad presenting a statistic stating that X percent of people die in the ER due to understaffing and slow treatment. Although interesting, there's a minimal chance consumers will remember this fact or be engaged to process it more deeply. In contrast, imagine a person telling viewers an awful story in which a husband had to watch his wife become increasingly sick and dangerously ill because the ER was slow and understaffed. The story goes on to provide contextual details to draw in viewers further and really allow them to feel as if they were in the moment at the ER. What makes the second advertisement more effective is the ability to provide a real and relatable context with emotion and depth that encourages the listener to empathize with the characters and the situation. The more experientially engaged persons are with the story and its message, the more motivated they are to continue to process information. This engaged processing of information translates then into a greater chance for the information in the commercial to connect with existing categories in the consumers' memory (nodes) to secure the information for later use, recall, and recognition. In fact, messages delivered as stories can be up to 22 percent more memorable than facts.[7]

Moreover, research shows that the brain can process images sixty times faster than words, and that 92 percent of consumers want brands to make ads that feel like a story.[8] Neuroscience research on advertising has studied facial coding of reactions by viewers while watching narrative versus information-based advertisements. According to the research, stories can attract more attention, are better liked, and can move people from being indifferent about one brand versus another to becoming greatly engaged with the message and the brand.[9]

Storytelling allows the creator to develop emotions and have the listener experience the setting rather than have a bunch of facts recited to them or, in the case of products, a list of benefits. Statistics support your points, while the story *is* your point.[10] Studies show that emotion-based ads are more effective than rational information-based ads. In a study undertaken across fourteen hundred successful advertising campaigns, 31 percent of the emotional campaigns reported large profit gains in comparison to similar gains in only 16 percent of the information-based campaigns.[11]

People also remember stories better, particularly when they have sticky information. As we discussed in chapter 4, the state of stickiness means that the consumer is engaged and motivated to spend time in the message.[12] The techniques for encouraging stickiness are addressed well in Chip Heath and Dan Heath's book *Made to Stick*[13] and include messages, according to Thomas Vogel, that are entertaining, memorable, and wrapped in personally relevant information.[14] Vogel outlines the key elements of a sticky idea as presented by the Heath brothers. For a message to be sticky it must be simple, unexpected, concrete (provide something tangible), credible, and emotional—presented in a story where the protagonist triumphs, inspiring the audience to take action.[15] As presented by Vogel,[16] the Heath brothers[17] use the Subway sandwich chain and Jared, the once-spokesperson for the company, to illustrate the elements of a sticky idea.[18]

Jared was a noncelebrity overweight person who started to eat at Subway to lose weight. The idea of wanting to eat healthy and lose weight is a *simple* one. However, the idea of eating at a fast-food restaurant to lose weight is *unexpected*. In ads, Jared would hold up his oversized pants to show that he had lost more than 200 pounds while eating Subway sandwiches (*concrete*). Jared was also *credible* to the target audience because he was just an average person wanting to lose weight like the rest of us. This point supports the next element of a sticky ad, which is the need to generate *emotional* connections between the audience, the protagonist, and the brand message. The goal of the narrative ad is to ensure the success of the protagonist while motivating the hearers to take action.

In this regard, storytelling is a very useful tool for the AIDA process, particularly in relation to increasing interest and desire. AIDA allows the encoder of the message to use emotions to connect with people's wants, needs, and motivations; the intent is to engage interest and raise desire by generating personal relevance, which enhances the likelihood of action.

SPECIFICITY AND STRUCTURE
IN NARRATIVE ADVERTISING

The actual design of a narrative ad follows a general story arc: an introduction (exposition), a conflict and rising action, a climax, and then falling action leading to a resolution.[19] But to make the story compelling and sticky, the choices of the key elements

of the story are critical. Vogel suggests that the plot, the characters (such as the protagonist), the theme, the conflict, and the
setting, as well as the language, tone, and pacing of the story
are all important details.[20] This is a critical point in reaching a
broad audience, because research suggests that the more specific,
detailed, and personalized the story, the broader the appeal. As
an example of the appeal of specificity, Ana Gotter compares the
following statements to assess which one is more interesting and
engaging, the generalized or the more specific story:

- "I had a hard time finding a date I was excited about."
- "Every date I went on was a disaster. One guy didn't have a
  job, one clearly hadn't showered in three days, one insulted
  me, and one literally lived in his mom's basement."

Gotter argues that the more specific the story is, the more
engaging and the better the chance of reaching a broader range
of people.[21] Narrative detail is not clutter; it is inviting to the
listener or reader. In advertising, however, the need for detail
in storytelling must be coupled with the need for an economy
of words and images because of a commercial's short length.
Every word must count.

Successful storytelling in advertising requires not only bringing an appropriate level of detail into the narrative but also
knowing your target audience to understand what types of stories will interest them and then crafting the story in such a way
as to have an emotional impact that also connects well with
your brand's values.[22] In other words, in narrative advertising
specificity is not a value for its own sake. The specific elements
used in a story-based ad must be appealing to and engaging for
a specific audience. Once advertisers study their target audience
in ways described in chapter 3, they have a familiarity with that
audience to suspect what will be appealing and engaging and are
ready to craft a message within a storytelling frame.

This specificity unfolds across the narrative arc. Evelyn
Timson argues that there are five elements of narrative structure that brands use to inspire consumers that parallel the five

movements of a traditional narrative arc (introduction or hook, conflict and rising action, climax, and falling action leading to a resolution) for the purpose of a narrative ad.[23] The first element is the *quest* that drives the story. What does the protagonist want and why? The protagonist should be a type of person to whom the consumer-audience can relate, someone who has wants and needs similar to the person you are trying to reach with your brand. For example, beauty products often try to make women feel more confident, and brands assert that they can help women achieve these goals, as shown in the ad with the protagonist experiencing the desired outcome.

The second element is *conflict* between the protagonist and the resolution of their quest. What is standing between the protagonist and their goal and why? In the case of beauty products it could be about what is stopping the protagonist from feeling confident, such as blemishes, dark circles, and so on.

The third element of narrative advertising Timson lifts up is *stakes*. What are the stakes at play in a quest being successful? For the protagonist's quest in the ad to matter to an audience, engaging emotion is critical—something must be at stake. The audience must be emotionally invested in the stakes to the point of cheering for the protagonist. This level of involvement and interest deepens the stickiness and motivation of the consumer to want to see what happens next. The questions for the storyteller to consider are as follows: Why is the quest important? What are the broader implications of the quest? Why should the audience care about the protagonist's success or failure?

Like all good stories, narrative ads need a *climax*. In the element of narrative climax, the story is drawing to a close and the conflict has been overcome with the stakes addressed. In developing a climax, the storyteller needs to consider how believable and relatable are the scenes heading to the climax. Should the end be a clear conclusion or left somewhat ambiguous?

The final element of a successful narrative ad is *emotional resolution*—the most important element necessary for a successful ad but also the most difficult to achieve. An advertisement must make a connection between the story and the

brand that consumers experience as authentic. People are looking for a strong and satisfying emotional resolution that is not
forced or awkward. One way Timson suggests connecting the
narrative to the brand is by making sure the values shared in
the story are similar to the brand's core values, which align
with consumer-held values (see the discussion of values in
chapter 3). Consider the Procter and Gamble (P&G) Olympic
commercial discussed earlier that shows mothers raising athletes through the ups and downs of wins, losses, and injuries.
Finally, in the climax of the story, the athletes overcome the
obstacles to win gold medals. Alone this ad is an emotionally
powerful story, but does it link the story to the brand? The ad's
most important element for the brand is the moment when the
athletes turn to their moms after winning, and P&G makes
the connection—"The hardest job in the world is the best job
in the world. Thank you, Mom. P&G Worldwide Partner"—
while displaying pictures of P&G products many mothers buy
and use. The emotional resolution is a moment of transferring
to the P&G brand the positive feelings the viewer has about
this story of mothers and their children. The understanding
that P&G and their viewers share these values makes that emotional transfer possible.

A humorous ad for Axe Body Spray titled "Soulmates"[24]
also illustrates all of the elements in effective narrative advertising just described.[25] The ad shows a young man appearing
in different recognizable eras across history (Ice Age, Pom-
peii, Arabia, the Old West, nineteenth-century London, the
Titanic, World War II, and the Vietnam War). In each scene,
a woman—his potential soulmate—catches his eye. Just as he
moves toward her, however, something occurs to keep them
apart, such as an earthquake, Mount Vesuvius erupting, being
hit over the head with a whiskey bottle, and being arrested.
Across all the scenes, the background music is the pop song
"One" ("One is the loneliest number"), which builds in volume as the ad progresses.

The opening Ice Age scene establishes the *quest* as a univer-
sal one—a man's search for his soulmate. In all nine different

scenes, the *conflict* is the same throughout: a disruption blocks the man from meeting his fated love. While the repetition of the conflict is humorous, it is also engaging, raising the *stakes* each time the man fails and each time the historical period draws closer to that of the contemporary viewer.

The *climax* is reached in a closing scene when the young man appears in a modern-day convenience store, takes Axe Body Spray off the shelf, and sprays himself. At this point the woman approaches him, instead of the reverse. Finally, the conflict is overcome. The *emotional resolution* occurs when the couple is shown walking away from the store. In the background a gas truck jackknifes into the gas pump and the store explodes. Had the young man relied on his own efforts instead of Axe, another epic crisis would have prevented them from being together. The words "Don't rely on fate" appear on screen followed by a close-up of Axe Body Spray containers. The goal is to create a sense of delight that viewers, especially young men, get from seeing the protagonist finally meeting the young woman. The delight is transferred to their own desires to meet their soulmate and to use Axe as a tool for helping them achieve their desire.

Overall, narrative advertising has proven to be a powerful technique to speak to an audience and motivate them to invite a brand or message into their life stories. While storytelling has long been effective in advertising, its importance is increasing because it especially works well with postmodern culture's rejection of outside authority and the move to make meaning based on experience. Instead of telling people what to do—the way information-based ads do—storytelling leads an audience down an engaging path and invites them to act in accordance with what they have experienced.

STORYTELLING IN SERMONS

Because storytelling is central to who we are as humans, that it plays such an important role across religious traditions is no surprise. Certainly, storytelling has been a key element of Christian proclamation since the days of Jesus teaching in parables and the four Gospel writers narrating their theology in biographical sermons.

As part of the traditional rhetorical approach to preaching that dominated for the last five hundred years, stories were used as "illustrations." The meat of the sermon was considered to be the exegetical and theological exposition offered by the preacher to persuade, offer insight to, or invite growth in the congregation. This exposition was often structured by a series of points, with the use of the word "points" indicating a primarily intellectual endeavor. Stories were used to "illustrate" such exposition; to make abstract points clear, concrete, and relatable; and to show the relevance of the sermon's message.

In the last half-century, due to the rise of the New Homiletic in the 1970s and 1980s, many preachers changed their approach to why and how we use stories in our sermons. Instead of seeing stories as a side dish or even garnish on the side of the plate, preachers recognized that listeners experienced stories as the sermon's main dish. Ask parishioners on Tuesday what they recall from Sunday's sermon, and it will not be Point 2.a.iii. They will recall the story of the arthritic grandmother struggling to get down to the floor of her porch to push Matchbox cars along the grain of the wood slats with her grandson, not the discourse on the nature of the economic Trinity. The New Homiletic taught preachers to offer congregations an *experience* of the gospel instead of a propositional argument about or from the gospel.[26]

It may look as if the New Homiletic abandoned exegetical, theological persuasive discourse, but this is not the case at all. Instead, this movement *reversed* the relationship between exposition and storytelling. In the place of stories serving expository points by following them with concrete examples, expositional discourse serves stories in sermons by setting them up to be heard and experienced in certain ways that are relevant to the congregation's existential concerns.

Stickiness on Sermonic Stories

Advertising's increased use of storytelling, especially when combined with elements of information-based ads, can help preachers sharpen their use of stories in sermons for offering an experience of some aspect of God's good news framed by informational-type exposition. We start with the elements that make a story sticky.

Sticky stories are *simple* and *concrete*. As we noted in the opening chapter, it is difficult for communicators to be heard in today's 24/7 multimedia world due to all the noise with which they must compete. The more complex the communication, the harder it is for receivers to hear the message *and* the more difficult it is for them to remember it even if it gets through. As with stories in thirty-second commercials, so with short stories that are part of a longer sermon. To have the potential to be heard, experienced, and remembered, sermonic stories need to be simple and concrete—but they need not be simplistic. Stories in service to the gospel need to have gravitas worthy of the subject matter of humanity's deepest concerns and God's expansive care for the world. But still the story's structure, number of characters, frame of reference, and so forth need to be of a small, manageable scale that the hearers can absorb or embrace.

Sermonic stories need something *unexpected* to be sticky. The story of salvation history itself is the foundation for such a narrative element in sermons: God's providential and salvific care for the very world that so often turns away from God constantly surprises us because it is so undeserved. While not all unexpected elements in sermonic stories must relate to God's character and activity, most should point in that direction, at least metaphorically. Too often we use stories in sermons to illustrate some small, passing point that really has little to do with the central theological, existential claim. If such stories are more vivid than ones showing the incarnate nature of the aspect of the gospel being preached, they are distracting instead of helpful.

For stories to help hearers experience the incarnate nature of the good news, they must be *credible*. When dealing with humanity's bad news (the itchy part of the sermon), preachers are very credible. The sin, injustice, frailty, suffering, and struggles of humanity are easy to show in ways that listeners believe and recognize. The problem is with the good news, the scratch of the sermon. Preachers have a difficult time finding simple, concrete stories that are believable in carrying the weight of God's mercy, justice, and calling. Good news stories can easily become Hallmark movies that fix all the problems of the world with a nice, neat, sentimental bow. People enjoy Hallmark movies because they are escapist and fun. Viewers are not, however, transformed by such movies. Because coming up with just the right story to carry the sermon's message is so hard, preachers often "show" the bad news but then just "tell" the good news, avoiding stories in the latter part of a sermon altogether.[27] This approach will not suffice. For congregations to experience God's good news in an *emotional* and transformative way, the good news in sermons needs to be shown to be true to their lives.

For a story to be credible and have emotion, it must have a *protagonist* with whom the congregation identifies and for whom the congregation roots. Such identification does not require that the protagonist and audience share identical characteristics. However, there must be enough similarity between protagonists and their situations and the hearers for the hearers to intuitively draw analogies to themselves and their lives. This is one reason famous people and saints of the church worked well as illustrations for sermons but do not work as protagonists in stories carrying the proclamatory weight of a sermon. Stories of saints and famous people may help make a point hearers can understand, but rarely will we identify with them as human beings like us. Hearers need protagonists who are on the same types of *quests* they are, who are struggling with a *conflict* similar to real conflicts the hearers experience in their own lives. That narrative conflict must have something significant at *stake* that resembles what is at stake in hearers' real lives. Thus, when an emotional connection between a true-to-my-life character and audience is formed, a positive resolution for the protagonist in the narrative points to the possibility of an analogous positive effect in the hearers' lives. The *climax* and *resolution* of the story are indicators of what is possible, even if only analogously so, in the hearers' lives.

When working on a sermon and considering whether a potential story will have the desired homiletical effect, preachers should ask themselves how members of their imagined focus group might hear, understand, and experience the story. Would each member of the group be able to identify with the protagonist, the protagonist's quest, and the conflict? If not, is there a way of showing or describing the character that would help form such an identification? Would the climax and resolution offer a twist that is unexpected and inviting while ringing credible and desirable to the listeners? How is the story best shaped for this group as an emotional embodiment of the sermonic message?

SERMONIC STORIES AND AIDA

Having considered the qualities of stories for sermons generally, it is helpful to recognize as well that stories have different purposes in different parts of a sermon. This issue was raised earlier in relation to stories embodying bad news/itch versus those embodying good news/scratch, but we can be more specific.

The opening of an AIDA-form sermon seeks to grab the congregation's *attention*. As a hook for the sermon, this section is likely brief. If using a story as part of the hook, it needs to be very short—perhaps not a full story so much as a glimpse at part of a scene. The goal is to foreshadow the topic of the sermon, which is yet to be named fully. A story at this point makes a promise about deeper engagement to follow while carefully avoiding fulfilling that promise. As such, the most important element of a story here usually is the *unexpected*. Introducing an unexpected element at the beginning of the sermon leads the congregation to want more of the message the preacher is offering.

Having grabbed the listeners' attention, the preacher next works to create in the congregation real *interest* in the sermonic topic and then deepen their *desire*. The topic introduced in the opening is problematized in increasingly significant ways. Stories in these two movements establish the hearers' emotional connection with the topic by showing that what is at stake is of relevance to the hearers. Embodying the itchy side of the sermon's message, these stories are usually more developed than those in the hook, but they still fall short of reaching a point of narrative climax that results in a resolution. In other words, these stories are still not full stories. The quest is not completed, the conflict not resolved. They can be part of a story that is finished in the closing section of the sermon (as it is in the sample sermon in the previous chapter) or self-standing scenes, but most important is that the narratives offer hearers protagonists with whom they can identify in the midst of a quest or conflict. The later in the sermon, the more these stories need to start hinting at a climax and resolution to come without giving away the ending.

The hinge from itch to scratch occurs in a dramatic way as the preacher shifts to present God's *action* on our behalf. As noted above, stories in this movement might complete part of a story introduced earlier in the sermon. In such a case, the hearers have already identified with the protagonist and the quest or conflict. The preacher need only remind the hearers of the character and their situation to reestablish that identification. Then the preacher can narrate the rest of the story to offer the congregation an experience of God's character and activity that brings a positive resolution to the story. More often, preachers introduce a new story at this point in the sermon, after the shift to the good news has been established. In such a case, the preacher needs to offer a characterization of the protagonists and their situation that invites hearers to identify with them. Because the hearers have already been emotionally involved in the topic (and with other protagonists in similar conflicts), it will be fairly easy to establish an emotional identification with the new protagonists. The emphasis in the story, therefore, must be on creating a credible and unexpected climax that the congregation can draw analogously into their own experience.

STORY-SERMONS

One way for preachers to harness the power of story in sermons is to preach story-sermons. While a narrative sermon is a sermon that follows a narrative logic (such as proposed by Lowry), a story-sermon is a sermon in which the whole of the sermon is a single story. Such sermons can offer the gospel with great emotional power yet should be used only occasionally and with restraint.

For a story-sermon to be engaging and have emotional impact, it must involve the elements discussed above: be a simple and concrete story in which a protagonist with whom the congregation can identify undertakes a quest with personal relevance for the congregation. The rising action, conflict, and climax should include unexpected but credible elements. But a story-sermon must be more than just engaging. To proclaim the gospel, it must be rooted in sound exegesis, offer theological commentary on an existentially relevant issue, and come to a resolution in the story world that invites hearers to recognize the potential for an analogous resolution for themselves.

The story-sermon presented here as an example tries to include these qualities and is based on the parable of the Vineyard Workers in Matthew 20:1–16:

> "For the kingdom of heaven is like a landowner who went out early in the morning to hire laborers for his vineyard. After agreeing with the laborers for the usual daily wage, he sent them into his vineyard. When he went out about nine o'clock, he saw others standing idle in the marketplace; and he said to them, 'You also go into the vineyard, and I will pay you whatever is right.' So they went. When he went out again about noon and about three o'clock, he did the same. And about five o'clock he went out and found others

standing around; and he said to them, 'Why are you standing here idle all day?' They said to him, 'Because no one
has hired us.' He said to them, 'You also go into the vineyard.' When evening came, the owner of the vineyard said
to his manager, 'Call the laborers and give them their pay,
beginning with the last and then going to the first.' When
those hired about five o'clock came, each of them received
the usual daily wage. Now when the first came, they thought
they would receive more; but each of them also received the
usual daily wage. And when they received it, they grumbled
against the landowner, saying, 'These last worked only one
hour, and you have made them equal to us who have borne
the burden of the day and the scorching heat.' But he replied
to one of them, 'Friend, I am doing you no wrong; did you
not agree with me for the usual daily wage? Take what belongs
to you and go; I choose to give to this last the same as I give to
you. Am I not allowed to do what I choose with what belongs
to me? Or are you envious because I am generous?' So the last
will be first, and the first will be last."

The sermon follows the logic of the parable to address the
question of theodicy, specifically the tension between God's
mercy and God's fairness. How do we reconcile the vineyard
owner's right to give the day workers who only worked an hour
the same amount he gave those who worked all day with the
result that some people were paid a twelfth of a denarius an
hour and others a denarius an hour. This passage is difficult for
many readers, and theodicy is an issue that goes to the core of
Christian theology and faith.

The existence of unexpected qualities is hinted at in the
sermon title itself, which appeared in the worship bulletin as
"Brooms, Justice, and Amazing Grace." The narrator of the
story is the boy Jackson Lewis Hillman, but the protagonist is
Mr. Masters, owner of the local broom factory—he is the one
struggling with the question of theodicy. The hook of the story
introduces the narrator and protagonist and the unexpected
conflict, the quest to find an appropriate interpretation of the
parable of the Vineyard Workers and thus to the question of

theodicy. The story is set in a fictional town in 1906. The fictional aspect and the distant setting allow the hearers to let down any defenses and move close into the story quickly.

> The first job I ever had was with the Masters Broom Company. It was the largest employer in Tinyville, Mississippi, where I grew up. The corporate slogan was "Our most satisfied customer is our last customer." The company was owned and run by Mr. Masters.
>
> Let's see, I was around thirteen when I went to work for the company, so I guess it was around 1906. I still remember my interview. Mind you, the opening was a part-time job at the bottom of the broom-making ladder. I wasn't applying for any of the glamorous jobs that paid well, like measuring out the amount of straw for each broom, or binding the straw, or cutting the straw ends so they were all even. I knew you would have to prove yourself before you got to deal with straw responsibility. I was applying for a job in the broomstick department. If I got the job I would be sanding every broom handle that went out of the Masters Broom factory. This wasn't unimportant work—I kept a lot of people from getting splinters. But it didn't directly impact the cleaning ability of the brooms the way the straw division did.
>
> So it was odd that even though I was only applying for a bottom-of-the-dust-pile position, the head of the company interviewed me. Evidently he, and not his foremen, hired every employee. I guess I remember it so well because it was so odd. Mr. Masters didn't ask me if I had previous work experience. He didn't ask me if I had ever worked with wood before. He didn't ask me if I had ever seen a broom. His questions were primarily religious. Not in the sense that he was basing whether or not I got the job on whether or not I was religious. He was asking about a religious question he had.
>
> "Mr. Jackson Lewis Hillman, how are you? I've known you since you were in diapers and here you are applying for a job in my plant. I hope your folks are doing OK. You tell your

mother that was a mighty pretty dress she was wearing at church on Sunday. And tell your daddy I've missed him over at Bonnie's Diner during coffee hour. He's got to get out of the office more. Well, enough small talk, let's see if you are Masters Broom Company material.

"What do you think of people who don't work for a living but then expect those of us who do to take care of them?"

I hadn't expected a question like that, but stuttered something in response like, "Well, I guess that's wrong. Everybody should work. My daddy works here in town, and Mama works at running the house and the little farm we have. Everybody should work. Why wouldn't they?"

"Just lazy," he said, "that's why. Some people are just lazy. Do you think God rewards laziness?"

"Sir, I don't guess I understand the question."

"Well, you were in church Sunday. You heard the preacher talking about God's grace and how it's free and such. He talked about deathbed conversion. Even at the very last moment, at the eleventh hour so to speak, God will forgive you and you go to heaven. Now that just doesn't seem fair to me. You and I spend our whole lives working hard at trying to be good people, right? And then some lazy sinner comes along at the last moment and says I'm sorry and gets exactly the same pay you and I get. Is that fair?"

"Well, I guess not," I said without having a clue how any of this related to sanding broomsticks.

"You know what song I hate?" he asked without any segue. "'Amazing Grace.' That song has done more to promote laziness in this world than anything I know. 'Amazing grace how sweet the sound. . . blah, blah, blah.' I think we ought to rewrite the words."

And then in the middle of the interview, Mr. Masters started singing [SING TO THE TUNE OF "AMAZING GRACE"]:

O God who's fair, how sick are those
who don't pull their share of the load.
Let them go down where they will roast,
and get what they are owed.

"It's just that I think God helps those who help themselves. I mean if God isn't fair, then the whole world doesn't make sense. Right?"

"I guess so," I said, and then I asked, "But what about that parable that Brother Gilmer was talking about on Sunday?"

Mr. Masters turned red-faced at this point.

"That's exactly what I'm talking about. No employer could really get away with paying someone who worked one hour the same amount he or she paid someone who worked a good day's work. And they shouldn't! It's not fair. And don't you think God is fair? There must be a translation problem with that parable or something! Jesus couldn't have claimed that everyone is equal regardless of the effort they put forward!"

All I could think to say was, "I didn't write the parable."

Now I don't want you to get the wrong picture of Mr. Masters. It wasn't that he was stingy or greedy and wanted to make a bunch of money and keep everyone else poor. It wasn't that he wanted to be rewarded by God while everyone else is punished. He really just couldn't conceive how God could epitomize both justice and grace at the same time. Either God is absolutely fair or God is completely forgiving, but God can't be both. And Mr. Masters was utterly convinced that God is fair. So he became obsessed with finding an alternative interpretation of the parable of the Householder and the Day Laborers, some way of seeing God as not rewarding the lazy the same way God rewards the hardworking, some way of taking grace out of the parable.

The quest has been announced, the conflict introduced. The itchy element of the parable has been named, and the theological core of the sermon foreshadowed. In case the hearers distance themselves from Mr. Masters too far and view him as some sort of Ebenezer Scrooge, the closing paragraph of the above section offers Jackson's sympathetic view of him. By doing so, the hearers are invited to sympathize with Mr. Masters as well and to claim his question as their own.

The next movement of the story-sermon primarily helps the hearers recognize how important the question of theodicy becomes for Mr. Masters, thus raising the stakes for investing in the question themselves. The section includes a retelling of the parable so that it sticks in the minds of the hearers, but this retelling is framed by other ways that Scripture and Christian thought raise the question of God's fairness.

A new setting is also introduced: Bonnie's Diner. The name of the restaurant foreshadows the introduction of a character who later serves to deepen the conflict in a way that pushes it to the point of climax and resolution.

> Every weekday around ten o'clock or so, Mr. Masters would go to Bonnie's Diner over on Maple Street for coffee and pastry. You know, most small towns have a place like Bonnie's. Early in the morning the farmers gather there for breakfast. Later in the morning the men who work in town gather for coffee and, well, gossip. Well, it got to be where the ten o'clock men hated to see Mr. Masters walk through Bonnie's door, because one way or another he would force the conversation to turn toward the issue of God's fairness. They'd be sitting there at the counter talking about the weather and Mr. Masters would say, "What do you think it means when the Bible says that God makes it rain on the just and the unjust alike? That doesn't seem fair to me." Or they'd be talking about Jamie Langford's illness, and he would raise the question, "Do you think sickness is God's way of punishing sinners and health is God's reward for righteousness?"
>
> Or they'd talk about the economy and he would assert, "Those who live right will do fine regardless of the shape of the economy. God blesses those who work hard. And God lets the lazy suffer the consequences of their own laziness: poverty. That's why that parable about the vineyard workers can't be right. You know, it says this vineyard owner goes out to the marketplace first thing in the morning and hires a bunch of men to help bring in his harvest. He promises them a standard day's wage for a standard day's work. But then he

goes back three hours later and finds some other guys there. 'What are you doing here?' he asks. 'You come on out to the vineyard and I'll pay you what's right for part of a day's work.' And then he goes out again three hours after that and then three more hours and then again when there is only one hour of work left in the day. When the day is done he has them paid starting with those who worked the least. To everyone's surprise, he pays these last ones a full day's wage, so those who worked all day expect more than the lazy ones got. But the owner pays them all exactly the same amount. When one of the ones who worked all day complained, as he ought to have, the vineyard owner says, 'Friend, didn't I pay you exactly what you agreed to? How can you complain? Can't I do what- ever I want with my money?' Now, I've just got to take the side of the worker in this case. The owner has not acted fairly. I couldn't run my business that way. And I don't believe God's business is run that way either. What do you guys think?"

And, of course, everyone would stare down at the counter, sip their coffee, and not say a word.

Having established the importance of the new setting for Mr. Masters's quest to unfold, the next section raises the stakes of the conflict when Bonnie challenges his logic in an existential, parabolic manner.

One morning Mr. Masters was taking his regular walk over to Bonnie's Diner for the coffee hour. When he turned off of Main Street onto Maple, he saw someone standing on the sidewalk in front of the diner. It was a man selling homemade brooms. The handles of the brooms were made out of tree branches and bent this way and that. They weren't sanded; in fact they still had the bark on them. The straw wasn't very sturdy, and the ends weren't very even. The man selling the brooms was an older Black man. He wasn't blind, but it was clear from the way he didn't really look at the world around him that he couldn't see much. And his clothes were thread- bare and had holes in them. He was wearing boots, but he didn't have any socks. And for someone selling a cleaning instrument, he wasn't very clean himself.

Mr. Masters started yelling at the man halfway down the block. "Hey, you! Boy! Get outta here! My company makes the brooms in this town, heck in this state. I pay taxes so that I can make and sell brooms. It's not fair for you to just tie some hay on the end of some rotten piece of wood you picked up off the ground and steal my business. It's a good thing Bonnie doesn't know you're out here. She would have called the sheriff!"

Not daring to look Mr. Masters in the eye, the man responded while staring down at the sidewalk, "Sir, Miss Bonnie is the one who said I could set up out here."

Mr. Masters burst into the diner.

"Bonnie, what in the . . . ? Why would you let this lazy bum sell brooms out in front of your store? Haven't I always been a good customer? Haven't I always tipped well? It's not fair you letting him steal my business."

"Oh, come on, Mr. Masters," Bonnie said. "Do you really think those four or five brooms he has out there are really going to hurt your profits? Besides, you're the one who convinced me I ought to let him sell out there."

"Me?! How in the . . . ? How did I convince you to let someone steal food from my mouth?"

"Well, it's that parable you keep talking about. I must have heard you recite it fifteen or twenty times in the last two and a half months. You know . . . the vineyard owner and the laborers he hires throughout the day and then pays them all the same. Well, I realized that it isn't about who gets into heaven. It isn't even really about the way God is. It's about the way things ought to be—you know, the world, here and now. And the way things ought to be is fair."

Mr. Masters couldn't help interrupting. "That's what I've been saying all along. Things ought to be fair."

Bonnie spoke back up: "Exactly! But you think fair would be if everyone in the parable got paid for the amount of work they did. I think fair would have been if all of the workers had gotten the chance to work all day in the first place. After all, if you think about it, not one of the people at the marketplace turned down the vineyard owner when they were invited to work. It's just that not all got the invitation from the start. Is it fair to penalize those who are missed in the beginning? Is it fair to blame them for being overlooked? I think the parable was Jesus' way of saying that God's grace is the correction of what is unfair. Grace is putting everybody at the same, level plane, giving everyone the same chance. And maybe that's what we are supposed to be all about. So when this gentleman asked me if he could sell brooms out front, I thought of your ranting and raving about the fact that God ought to be fair, and I decided to give him the best shot at a fair shake I could. I let him try to sell to my customers."

Mr. Masters tried to speak up and give a response, but Bonnie must have thought she had heard all he had to say during the last two and a half months. So she turned away from the counter, picked up a rickety ol' homemade broom and started sweeping.

Bonnie's reinterpretation of the parable is the climax of the story-sermon. She offers a reading that goes against the preacher's concern about deathbed conversions quoted in the opening of the story and against Mr. Masters's argument that mercy and justice cannot be reconciled. She turns the view of fairness and mercy on its head and claims that God's mercy is seen when the world is fair in the first place. That is what God's reign is; that is what it looks like when God's will is done on earth as it is in heaven.

Bonnie's answer does not erase the whole problem of theodicy (Why do people suffer if God is all-knowing [i.e., is aware of the suffering], all-loving [i.e., cares about those suffering], and all-powerful [i.e., is able to alleviate the suffering]?) But then that is too much to expect of any single sermon. What Bonnie's answer does is offer Mr. Masters and those who have identified with him a piece of the puzzle—one simple, concrete, but not simplistic way of thinking about one aspect of the issue.

In the resolution of the narrative arc, Mr. Masters is now left to appropriate this new understanding of the parable, this new understanding of God's fairness:

> Since the conversation was obviously over, Mr. Masters got up to leave, with sort of a dazed look on his face.
>
> He stepped out of the diner into the morning light and paused for a second. Then he walked over to the man selling handmade brooms, and he said, "Excuse me, sir. What's your name?"
>
> "It's Andrew, Mr. Masters."
>
> "Well, Andrew, I wanted to say that I'm sorry about my rudeness a few minutes ago. I was wondering if I could, well, you know, buy a broom."
>
> Andrew sold him a broom and Mr. Masters turned to walk off, but then he stopped and said, "If you come by my factory later this afternoon, I'll have a job for you if you want one. It'll pay what everyone else gets."
>
> "Thank you, Mr. Masters. I could certainly use steady work. I'll be there."
>
> "Good, I'll see you at the factory. And call me Peter."
>
> And then Peter walked off down the road humming: [BEGIN HUMMING "AMAZING GRACE," AND SIGNAL THE CONGREGATION TO JOIN IN. SIT DOWN WHILE THE HUMMING FINISHES.]

The conclusion to the story shows the conversion of Mr. Masters and invites the congregation to experience the same sort of conversion in their own lives. Mr. Masters offers God's mercy to Andrew in the form of the chance to earn a fair wage. But Mr. Masters embraces this new vision of fairness in even stronger terms: at the beginning of the twentieth century, Jim Crow was alive and well. Yet Mr. Masters promises to pay this Black man the same amount he pays all his employees, shifts from calling him "boy" to calling him "sir," and invites him to address him by his first name, Peter. The name Peter, the last word of the story-sermon, evokes the memory of the chief disciple who consistently misunderstands Jesus' teachings but ends up becoming the rock on which the church is built. This same Peter is Andrew's brother.

CREATIVITY AIDS FOR PREACHERS

Thus far we have discussed the role of stories in individual sermons—the qualities that make for strong homiletical stories and how to use them in different parts of the sermon or as the whole of a sermon. But how are preachers to come up with these stories week after week, month after month, year after year? Here again, we can learn from advertising. What practices do advertising agencies use to enhance creativity in their regular work to design engaging ads?

In this case, advertising itself has learned techniques from other disciplines. What makes the creative process in advertising different from, say, an artist's process of painting a picture is that the ideas created for an ad must sell a brand by being relevant to a particular target audience. This situation is similar to a sermon offering a particular sermonic claim to a specific congregation on a given occasion.

In advertising, a "creative team" uses these techniques learned from other disciplines to assemble ads and formulate ad campaigns. Preachers working on a sermon alone can adapt some of these techniques, however, similar to the way we suggested adapting the use of focus groups for preaching. Preachers might find two types of exercises in particular helpful. The first can assist them in developing their creativity generally. The second exercise can provide creative boosts when preachers are looking for stories and other creative elements for a particular sermon.

Exercises to Increase Creativity

While some people are naturally more creative than others, everyone can increase their creativity in order to generate unique ideas. Paul Suggett provides fifteen exercises to practice one's creativity skills that are effective, interesting, and fun.[28] We include a few here that can be especially useful to preachers.

One suggestion is to work on *designing a twenty-seventh letter for the alphabet.* You need to consider what it would sound like or look like. Seminary training primarily leads preachers to think about the theological, exegetical, and existential content of their sermons. But good preachers also think about how their content sounds, how it resonates in the hearers' ears. Exercises like this focus preachers' creativity on sound.

Another idea is to *invent a new sandwich,* maybe even based off a specific celebrity or other famous person. Creators would need to consider what ingredients would be attractive to consumers while also addressing key attributes of the person it would be named after. Preachers might adapt this exercise to create a sandwich (or some other dish) based off a biblical character or a figure from church history who would be attractive to different segments of their congregation. While silly, the exercise builds up the creative muscle for drawing connections between contemporary hearers and ancient people with whom preachers want them to identify.

One technique especially relevant to storytelling is to try to *write a six-word story.* Many are familiar with Ernest Hemingway being asked to write a complete story in just six words for which he created: "For sale: baby shoes, never worn." Preachers need to be able to offer central imagery and stories for their sermon using an economy of words. To expand this exercise, preachers might regularly read and try their hand at writing microfiction (usually defined as stories three hundred words or less).[29]

Another fun and helpful exercise to help strengthen your creativity muscles is to *come up with a gadget that the world is missing.* For example, "Flip-it!" was created to fit on the lid of most condiment bottles and has legs to stand the bottle upside down in order to get the very last bit of product out of the bottle.[30] This exercise can help preachers build the creativity muscles needed to identify an itch and shape the proper scratch for it while avoiding clichéd responses.

In addition to these exercises proposed by Suggett, preachers can also benefit from tips for strengthening the creative mind offered by Thomas Vogel throughout his book *Breakthrough Thinking: A Guide to Creative Thinking and Idea Generation.*[31] Vogel's focus is more on exercises dealing with everyday activities and specific tasks. In regard to everyday strengthening ideas, he argues that people who want to think creatively need to read as much as possible while limiting time watching television. On the experiential side, he stresses the importance of trying new things, like learning another language or engaging in a new hobby, and suggests we need to find reasons to laugh—and when stuck in a rut, work on clearing the mind with exercise.

Exercises When Looking for a Creative Element of a Sermon

In addition to using the above practices to build creative muscle in general, creative teams in advertising agencies need some help from time to time when they are trying to move from an OK idea to that unique idea that promises to engage a target audience and help them connect with a product and purchase it. Preachers can use these types of help when they are trying to free their minds to come up with just the right idea, story, metaphor, or turn of phrase needed to undergird the central message of a sermon on which they are working.

The authors of a popular advertising textbook provide a simple *six-step model outlining the creative process.*[32] The six steps are

1. Immersion—learning everything about the relevant material.
2. Ideation—looking at the issue from multiple perspectives.
3. Brainfog—hitting a blank wall.
4. Incubation—a stage where you turn off your direct focus on the issue and let your unconscious mind turn on by going for a run or engaging in some other activity.

5. Illumination—the aha moment when the idea comes, often while not consciously thinking about the problem.
6. Evaluation—consideration to assess if the creative idea is on strategy to reach the stated goals.

This process can be applied to sermon preparation. When preachers begin looking for just the right story or such for a movement of their sermon, they should have already passed through the first step, *immersion*. They have done their exegesis, theologically reflected on the issue raised by the text, considered the existential connection of the issue for their congregation, and shaped a central sermonic claim or message. This work is deepened and sharpened with the *ideation*. The preacher needs a story for a specific moment in the sermon and intensely considers a variety of possibilities from different angles. However, then often comes the *brainfog*. Students of creativity used to think of brainfog as a problem, but now thinkers consider it a normal and important step of the creative process. Having a dry spell or hitting a blank wall signals the moment when one should lay aside consciously working on the problem (left-brain activity) to allow the (right) brain to engage the problem at the unconscious level: *incubation*. Alternating between intense focus and incubation often leads to a moment of *illumination*. Recognizing the necessity of brainfog and this alternation should remind preachers that bringing true creativity into their sermons requires time. But an aha moment is not the end of the process. The first aha that a preacher has when looking for the right story can often fall short of a sermon's full potential. Thus, *evaluation* is needed. Does the story fit with central claim of the sermon? Does it fit at the particular point of the sermon in which a story is needed? Are the characters and action relatable for the congregation?

Beyond engaging this broad creative process, preachers can borrow several exercises from advertisers to help generate creative ideas. One exercise is called *random input*.[33] The goal is to help direct one's thinking away from habitual concepts and perceptions. The technique can be implemented in several different ways, such as selection of a random word from the dictionary or using a music shuffle to have a random song selected. Let's consider the dictionary option. Preachers who are stuck in trying to find imagery for a specific part of their sermon can open a dictionary and take a random word from a random page. Then they work to try to connect the word with situation or issue they are trying to bring to life in the sermon. It is fine if the result is contrived, because the goal of the exercise is not actually to use the word in the sermon but to free up the mind from where it was previously stuck so that it can enter new areas of creative thinking.

Related to random input is a *mind map* (see Figure 5.1), in which one puts a word or concept with which they are dealing in the center of a page and then generates as many ideas that come to mind in relation to the original topic area. The end result should look like a chaotic flowchart sprouting off in all directions.

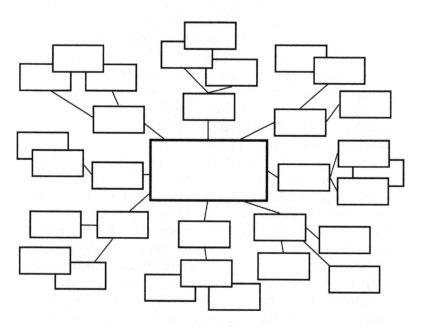

Figure 5.1

This is not simply brainstorming about the central topic but intentionally chasing rabbits down different trails. As an example, imagine an advertising team writing the word "Ford" in the center and then branching off from there along one of the paths. Perhaps the center leads out to the following words, car, economy, not flashy, young adult, loan, debt, bank, pig, farm, hay, bugs, bug spray, camping, fish, allergy, and so on. In using this technique the team has come up with several different ideas and paths to follow to which they might not originally have had access. Preachers can play with mind maps for any idea (itch or scratch) on which they are stuck in a sermon (greed, joy, worry, Holy Spirit, mercy, justice, generosity, salvation, church, Samaritan, healing). The intense exegetical and theological work preachers have already done will naturally and perhaps unconsciously frame how the mind map begins so that time is not wasted going in unhelpful directions. But the freedom of the mind map also helps the preachers' imaginations not be limited by that frame in ways that will lead to missing the perfect idea.

Another technique to generate unique and impactful messages is to engage in *reversal*.[34] This is an exercise in trying to come at a creative problem from the opposite side. The example Vogel gives is related to advertisers wanting to create a message around customer satisfaction. In order to look at the topic from a different perspective, the creative team can consider experiences when they have had low customer satisfaction. Once they have generated many ideas around what might cause poor customer satisfaction, they can examine the brand or company to see areas where it excels in any of these areas where the company can then refocus their ad's message. This exercise fits very well with sermons structured to move from itch to scratch. In truth, it is usually not difficult for preachers to find images that work well in the itchy part of the sermon—preachers can relay bad news all day long because it is so pervasive. It is difficult, however, to come up with stories or images that work on the scratch side of the sermon that are worthy of God's good news. Using reversal, preachers can take the kind of story they need (scratch), imagine its opposite, and then try to reverse-engineer the story. This story itself may not be appropriate (since it is likely fictional) but can lead one to see anew the perfect story.

Another way to jar the mind into new territory is to ask *What if?* questions.[35] These should be far-fetched questions such as, "What if babies could talk?" In taking this approach, the potential range of ideas expands into new realms, allowing for a new and unique way to convey the message. Recall the famous ad during the Super Bowl by E-Trade that used babies talking about how easy it was to make a trade using E-Trade.[36] The advertisement was unique, entertaining, and memorable while conveying well the ease of using E-Trade. Preachers can use this technique when trying to find memorable ways to show the good news in a sermon. Imagine working on a sermon on one of the passages where Jesus eats with sinners and tax collectors and the sermon is going to deal with the tension between God's unconditional love and cheap grace. What if Jesus were invited to give the keynote address at a dictator and terrorist convention?

A final exercise creative teams use is Edward de Bono's *Six Thinking Hats*.[37] De Bono developed six hats, each having a different color to represent thinking from a certain perspective. Each person in a group is assigned a particular metaphorical hat to wear and is expected to contribute to the creative discussion from the perspective of that hat:

- The *white hat* requires one to think from an information and knowledge base.
- The *red hat* has the person focused on intuition, emotions, and feelings.
- The *black hat* has the person approach the issue with caution to consider what might go wrong or what obstacles might arise.
- The *yellow hat* promotes positive thinking and encourages thinking about as many positive associations and ideas as possible.

- The *green hat* is about possibilities out of our comfort zone and pushes people to consider the "what ifs" and imagine anything.
- Finally, the *blue hat* is unique from the others in that the person wearing it controls the thinking process for the group members and ensures that each is being true to the characteristics of the specific color hat while also keeping time.

For use by an individual preacher, a five-hat process is proposed. In trying to come up with a creative idea for a sermon, preachers could give equal time to considering the topic from each of the following perspectives: information, emotion, caution, positivity, and what-ifs. One or two of these will likely show the most promise quickly and can be given more time.

6

Advertising Campaigns and Cumulative Preaching

Thus far we have focused primarily on what preachers can learn from the advertising world as they shape individual sermons. While preachers trust that the Holy Spirit is active in the sermonic event, they recognize that the individual sermon is limited in the effect it can have on a congregation. Instead, God uses preachers to shape Christian faith, identity, practices, and ethics over the course of sermon upon sermon, Sunday after Sunday, month after month, year after year. To conclude this experiment, then, we look beyond the individual thirty-second commercial and consider what preachers might learn from broader advertising campaigns about cumulative approaches to preaching.

ADVERTISING CAMPAIGNS

An *advertising campaign* is "a specifically designed strategy that is carried out across different mediums in order to both achieve results and to increase brand awareness, sales and communication."[1] Put differently, it is "a series of ads that are all designed to accomplish a single goal or revolve around a core message."[2] While an individual ad is targeted toward a narrow target market, campaigns can be narrow or broad depending on the intended appeal and purpose of the product or service being advertised. For instance, campaigns for prescription drugs will have a narrow target audience struggling with a specific medical condition, but those promoting a retail store chain with a wide range of products will strive to promote the brand to audiences crossing over different segmentations. A campaign, then, is like an umbrella, having a single idea or theme that covers a series of different but related advertisements placed across varied media as appropriate to reaching the target market(s).

Two elements of campaigns that are worth exploring for our homiletical purposes concern the fact that they are focused by a *common objective with a unified theme* and the rollout of the different advertisements and other promotional efforts is intentionally *coordinated*.[3]

Advertising campaigns are designed to meet a specific objective or a set of objectives. It might seem obvious that the end goal for every advertisement or campaign is sales, and in a sense this is true. But this may be an indirect, long-term goal with other direct goals contributing to it. A campaign might focus on raising brand awareness, generating interest, or helping build loyalty. There are many outcomes that a campaign might be trying to fulfill, with individual advertisements each contributing to the overall desired result as well as the varied media channels used.

The most important element of an effective advertising campaign is continuity.[4] All of the various components of the campaign must work together to achieve the campaign's goal. Attention to continuity means that the various advertisements and other promotional techniques (public relations, sponsorships, product placement, social media, etc.) have an identifiable common theme and a unified message to viewers.

Continuity does not mean conformity, however, and in fact conformity across a campaign will hurt a campaign's efforts.[5] Conformity can breed boredom and decrease interest. Every individual contact a campaign makes with consumers must grow out of the common theme and contribute to the unified message, but each should also function as a stand-alone selling tool. The execution of the campaign's theme and message (i.e., the story it is trying to tell) can vary significantly from ad to ad. Continuity without conformity allows the advertiser to layer similar (but not identical) information in different ways to continue to attract attention and deepen interest while sending an overall similar cumulative message about the brand through the different advertisements and media channels.

A way advertisers enhance continuity while avoiding conformity is to keep the concepts of extendibility and repeatability in mind.[6] In the former, you want to use a similar theme and common elements to convey your message across different media channels. In the latter you want to create messages that convey your overall brand message but execute the advertisements in different ways, which when put together tell a story but can stand alone as well. An example given is the famous "Got Milk" campaign.[7] While individual ads used different celebrities and the advertising used many different media channels from bus signage to magazine and television ads, the underlying theme and visual use of a milk mustache was the same to help achieve the overall campaign goals.

Typically, campaign goals relate to growing the brand. A campaign may introduce a new brand such as Tesla, an innovation for a brand such as adding a whitening ability for a toothpaste that has been around fighting cavities for years, or repositioning of a brand such as Old Spice from one used by an older generation to a cutting-edge product among young men.

Travelers Insurance has a campaign that exemplifies well how differences between the function of individual advertisements work together to create consistency in tone and theme. The "Red Umbrella" campaign, using the tagline "It's Better under the Umbrella," was designed to convey the overarching message that with Travelers Insurance you are covered. Travelers Insurance has been associated with the umbrella logo since the 1870s but in recent years has made it central to the brand's campaign.[8]

Travelers has worked to identify with consumers by developing a storytelling platform with an emotional connection around scenarios of when insurance would be important.[9] Through a series of different ads placed in a variety of media outlets, Travelers has been able to reach its varied target segments. One set of ads focuses on small businesses and how Travelers has you protected for this generation and those in the future if a fire or natural disaster should strike. Another set of ads focuses on the individual family and how Travelers has your family covered for whatever accidents may occur in the house or while driving.[10]

Another example of a rebranding campaign involves the sixty-year-old cereal brand in Canada called Shreddies. It is a cereal that is 100 percent whole grain and comes in brown squares. Sales were declining, but focus group research showed that consumers still liked the brand. The product did not need to be changed, but it did need to be rebranded to regain consumers' attention. An advertising agency developed a revival campaign promoting new "diamond"-shaped Shreddies. The ads were humorous because it was obvious to consumers that there was nothing new about the actual product at all: the new diamond-shaped Shreddies were just the square Shreddies turned on their side.

The campaign utilized several different advertisements and media channels in order to reach consumers effectively. Media channels included street advertising, TV commercials, print ads, a website, and a new package design. Ads across all the various media strictly adhered to the unified message and theme (continuity), but different media were chosen to execute that message in novel ways (avoiding conformity). For example, TV ads provided humorous, obviously fake footage of people in focus groups testing the diamond-shaped Shreddies and saying how they tasted better than the original square-shaped Shreddies. The website, however, provided information about "new technology" allowing for making the geometrically superior diamond-shaped Shreddies cereal.

Through this advertising campaign and varied message executions, the brand experienced an 18 percent market-share increase in the first month, while also winning several awards.[11]

This is a great example of the power of an advertising campaign to add value to a brand without any change to the product, simply by altering consumers' perceptions through entertaining and varied storytelling.

Developing campaigns that use different media to convey stand-alone messages that in turn cumulatively achieve the unified goal of the campaign requires significant *coordination*. In today's landscape the complexity of media planning continues to grow as media opportunities expand and user-generated content increases. However, advertisers use the same tried-and-true tools to move forward in planning messages and placement of ads among expanding media. For example, everything still starts with identifying a target audience and often focusing on the demographic characteristics of that audience, such as age, gender, marital status, and occupation. Advertisers determine where the identified audience frequents, the media they use and how they use it, and the Internet sites they visit and radio stations the listen to in working to develop the touch points for their advertising messages.

Beyond the more traditional media outlets of television, radio, print, and billboards, advertisers can also use public relations, Internet marketing, social media, direct marketing, product placement in television shows or movies, and event activations. They can use options such as sponsoring events, contests, discount coupons, or co-promotions with companies like Groupon or Foursquare. Advertisers also consider how they might advertise in the actual stores where the brand is sold, how to get the sales force in the store to promote the brand, and even what atmosphere and music might enhance sales. Every touch point used in advertising campaign to reach consumers must be coordinated with continuity of the overall brand message and campaign objective to be achieved.

The Old Spice campaign mentioned earlier is a great example of continuity and coordination that led to excellent results for the brand. Old Spice was a seventy-five-year-old brand heading toward extinction when it came out in 2010 with the now famous "The Man Your Man Could Smell Like" campaign. Isaiah Mustafa, a former NFL star, was the shirt-less six-packed actor in the ad shown in a towel getting into a shower. The ad was targeting women who buy deodorant and body wash that men tend to just use in the shower, while informing both male and female targets that now there is Old Spice Swagger for men. Using media channels and social media outlets, Old Spice was able to reach its new target market rang-ing from eighteen to thirty-four years of age to compete with the Axe brand and step away from the previous forty- to sixty-year-old mature man. The main message of the ad was that anything was possible "when your man smells like Old Spice and not a lady."[12]

Old Spice body wash sales increased 107 percent with more than 40 million views on YouTube within thirty days of the start of the campaign.[13] After the initial successful launch of the advertisement and consumers chatting and writing all over the Internet about the brand, Old Spice began to expand its touch points to interact with their fans. Old Spice allowed consumers and celebrities to ask the Old Spice guy questions, for which the ad agency made 180 video responses. The brand's YouTube channel more than doubled in subscribers to 150,000, while Twitter followings jumped 2,700 percent and 800 percent for Facebook.[14] While the various touch points provided different content, they all flowed out of and reinforced the same theme and tone of the campaign. This coordinated effort allowed Old Spice to become a part of the popular culture again, becoming the number-one selling brand for men's body wash. In 2013, the company expanded the campaign and included two more ads related to shave gel products. In just two weeks, these indi-vidual ads garnered 7.6 million views.[15] In the end, the conti-nuity of a unified theme using coordinated messages through each of the touch points, as well as timely interaction with mes-sages, allowed for successful rebranding.

However, not only must advertisers coordinate how ads in a campaign create different kinds of touch points and be concerned with continuity across the diversity of those touch points, they must also coordinate what level of frequency of ads appearing to its target market(s) they consider effective. *Effective frequency* is the "average number of times a person must see or hear a message before it becomes effective. In theory, effective frequency falls somewhere between a minimum level that achieves awareness and a maximum level that becomes overexposure, which leads to wearout [*sic*]."[16]

Determining effective frequency for a particular advertising campaign is complicated by the fact that not every contact a consumer has with a campaign is equal.[17] Some contacts may involve close attention to a narrative commercial and others only a passing glance at a picture on the side of a bus. Both methods are made more effective by being combined with the other. Different types and levels of exposure to a brand reinforce a common message to consumers without pushing them away.

The optimal frequency for a particular campaign depends to a great extent on the context of the message. Generally, research suggests anywhere from three up to seven times is good for the consumer to hear, engage, and remember a message.[18]

Brands once engaged and at the top of consumers' memory, however, can be forgotten. Sutherland and Sylvester remind us that often memory failure is less from poorly storing information in memory and more from the "inability to retrieve" the information due to other learning that has taken place since receiving the initial material.[19] This human characteristic is why advertisers of famous brands such as Coke undertake entertaining, reminder advertising to engage with consumers without a concern to offer new brand information. Here, too, wearout must be avoided. There is a fine line between reminding consumers of your brand and consumers becoming tired of your message.

In this case we must consider two kinds of advertising wearout: campaign wearout and ad execution wearout.[20] Sometimes an advertiser may have a great campaign concept, but individual ad executions have become old and have lost their ability to generate awareness, interest, and desire. Nike has been able to avoid this. Their "Just Do It" campaign started in 1988 and continues today. The advertising executions to convey that message, however, have changed with the times and shifted target audiences.

CUMULATIVE PREACHING

Being concerned with the cumulative effects of preaching is not new to the church.[21] The liturgical calendar and the resulting lectionary push the church to think cumulatively about the cycle of worship, liturgical themes (especially christological themes organizing the half of the year stretching from Advent through Pentecost), and the flow of Scripture readings (the Revised Common Lectionary especially attends to this cumulative effect of readings from parts of the canon other than the Gospels in Ordinary Time).[22] In recent decades, many churches have broken from the liturgical calendar and the lectionary to various degrees in shaping worship and sermon series that stretch a locally chosen theme over the course of a number of weeks.[23] Looking at cumulative approaches to preaching through the lens of advertising campaigns can enhance both of these approaches.

Advertising campaigns can have short-term or long-term goals. Introducing a new product or rebranding a product (such as the earlier Shreddies example) is a short-term-focused campaign that hopefully has indirect long-term effects in terms of reestablishing the brand in the marketplace. Longer-term-focused campaigns are often less about creating immediate effects, such as a boost in sales, and more about maintaining a brand's market share while creating sustained awareness of and loyalty to a brand, such as with Coca-Cola.

Preachers and worship planners usually think about cumulative preaching in terms of short-term strategies. How might sermons on the Lenten epistle lessons be focused on baptism to create a thematically consistent season and therefore sharpen the worshipers' experience of the good news in relation to the purpose and movement of Lent? How might a four-week sermon series in September use a back-to-school theme to reintroduce four basic tenets of Christian faith? Preachers also, however, need to think about the long-term effects of their preaching ministry.

In a postmodern era (see chapter 2), fewer preachers are willing to claim to have *the* theological outlook to which all of their congregants should hold. Still, though, they want to help their parishioners shape a broad, consistent Christian world-view and Christian identity that define the core of their lives. Such a goal is not achieved in the course of a single sermon or a short sermon series, no matter how effective. Slow and steady wins the true homiletical race. How do sermons during Lent this year build on what was done last year and the year before to ground and expand the congregation's broad sense of their baptismal identity? How might repeating variations on a series in September every year deal with basics of Christian theology in ways that invite newcomers into the conversation and deepen longtime members' engagement with those basics?

The principles guiding an advertising campaign can be helpful for preachers when thinking about short- and long-term cumulative preaching. In both limited series and preaching across time, it is important to focus on a *common objective with a unified theme*. In a sermon series, this overarching focus should be fairly tight. Too often churches come up with a catchy, punny title or an acronym for a series and then force content into it. Instead preachers should develop the theological, existential, or scriptural focus—or all three—and then figure out creative ways to market the series. The focus for the series could be on theology, spiritual health, a book of the Bible, a social justice issue, denominational identity, an emphasis of a liturgical season, and so forth. Then preachers look at the issue through different lenses throughout the series and avoid series that are divided into progressive parts.

This approach adheres to the advertising campaign's principle of maintaining continuity across the campaign while resisting conformity. Every individual sermon offered to hearers as part of a series must grow out of the common theme and contribute to the unified, overarching message, but each should also function as a stand-alone proclamation of God's good news. After all, some members of the church will only hear part of the series.

Preachers can apply in two ways the principle of having a common objective with a unified theme to their wider, ongoing preaching ministry. First, preachers need to be able to name what they understand to be the core of the gospel in a sentence or two in ways that avoid traditional theological clichés. In a sense this would be an expression of what a preacher considers as the core problem of human existence and God's foundational response to that problem.[24] Evangelical preachers have a different gospel core than liberationist preachers. Baptists disagree with Lutherans. Preachers shaped by Western culture may offer a different answer than those in the Global South. Differences among preachers is not a problem. But the same preacher offering conflicting gospels is.

Preachers need to offer their congregation a unified, consistent theological worldview over the course of their preaching ministry with that community. Of course, the topics on which each person preaches from Sunday to Sunday, season to season, year to year, will (and should!) vary significantly. Over the course of a preaching ministry, one should seek continuity without conformity: an overarching theology approached from many different homiletical roads with many different stops along the way.

No one preaches the gospel on any given Sunday—not the whole of the gospel, that is. In one sermon, preachers offer hearers a glimpse of a small piece of the giant gospel puzzle. Small does not mean insignificant; it simply means that the infinitely expansive nature of God's grace and justice cannot be contained in a sermon, a sermon series, or even in the entirety of anyone's preaching ministry. Small glimpses are all we have. Still, small glimpses that preachers intentionally work on to offer a cumulative, panoramic view of God's nature, will, and work lead congregations into greater knowledge of, experience of, and relationship with the mystery of the Divine than do sermons over time without any concern for continuity.

The second way preachers can apply the advertising campaign principle of having a common objective with a unified theme to their wider, ongoing preaching ministry is with smaller recurring themes and issues they want to raise with a congregation, especially issues that involve significant changes in some of the ways hearers think, feel, and behave. Every preacher knows of a multitude of such themes and issues in their congregation and over time can and should focus on several of them. Which ones receive more weight depends on preachers' priorities, their sense of how important the issue or theme is generally, and how critical it is for their specific congregation. This distinction raises the issue of *effective frequency*. How many times must a preacher raise such an issue for people to really hear it and be effected by it? Too few times and the gospel message effects no transformation. Too often or too close together, and some parishioners' defenses go up higher. Repetition is essential, but too much and a congregation can feel beat up instead of inspired or challenged. Wearout is as real in homiletical situations as it is in advertising.

One way to avoid such wearout is for preachers to realize that there are different ways to expose a congregation to an issue that needs sustained attention. At one point the preacher might preach a whole sermon on the issue, introducing it as a topic of importance for the church collectively and its members individually. At another time the preacher might present a sermon series on the issue and deal with it from different angles, avoiding conformity. In between and beyond, the preacher might bring up the issue directly in expository discourse or indirectly in a story in sermons dealing with other matters altogether.

As an example, let us recall the case-study sermons in the previous chapters. While each sermon dealt with very different Scripture texts, central messages, and themes, each one included an element that addressed race. In the sermon on the peaceable kingdom, the issue was raised with reference to historical violence against Native Americans and Russell Compton's willingness to converse with a KKK Grand Wizard as part of his commitment to racial justice. In the graduation sermon dealing with worship, diversity, and unity, the story about Dan Whitsett's resistance to segregation gave hope to the preacher facing racism in the church years later. In the story-sermon about Peter Masters's concern about God's justice, the man selling brooms on the street was African American, and the two ended up having a different relationship than was common in the early twentieth century. None of the sermons were about race. But if a preacher was convicted about dealing with race in a significant manner, keeping the spotlight on it is a prophetic action that can cumulatively lead a congregation to a point of addressing the issue in a more direct fashion.

Of course, preachers attend to cumulative strategies not just to deal with controversial issues. Similar to the goal of rebranding a product in order to reclaim a better market share, sometimes preachers want to reclaim a lost theological or biblical theme. For instance, eschatology is extremely important in the New Testament. Hardly a paragraph passes without revealing the New Testament authors' apocalyptic worldview, but this leaning is lost on much of the church in the twenty-first century. Imagine a preacher seeking to reclaim for eschatology its rightful place in the church's thought and outlook without interpreting biblical eschatological references literally, given that two thousand years have passed without Christ returning on a surfboard in the clouds.

The preacher could use Advent each year to repeatedly introduce the concepts related to eschatology as well as practices and attitudes of piety related to it (e.g., expectation, keeping watch, holding on to hope). The lectionary assigns to the first Sunday of every year a reading from the eschatological discourses in one of the Gospels. Focusing on this text year after year can invite the congregation to view Advent as an eschatological season instead of just a pre-Christmas season. Repeated sermonic language each year can slowly become the vocabulary of the congregation. The preacher might start the Advent 1 sermon each year wishing the congregation a happy new year, explain that this day marks the beginning of the Christian liturgical calendar, and then quickly move to how we Christians begin our year at the End with a capital E. The preacher can explain the already–not yet of eschatology in terms of hearers already experiencing God's salvation individually but the world has yet to see it fully manifested. Thus an eschatological existence is one in which we celebrate God's grace in our lives but express a holy dissatisfaction with the strife, suffering, injustice, and violence in the world. The experience of shaping one's life in relation to what we have already received and what we yet long for can be repeatedly illustrated with the same metaphor of driving down a country road at night. In long stretches of darkness, a driver turns on the high beams and edges toward the middle of the road. But when heading up a hill, the driver sees the spray of headlights on the other side of the hill and immediately turns down the high beams and moves over into the appropriate lane. That moment of already experiencing and responding to the headlight beams from the other car but not yet meeting the car fully is what constant, eschatological existence is like.

Advent 1, then, becomes the annual launching of an ongoing rebranding campaign concerning Christian eschatology. The annual theme on Advent 1 can shape the whole of an Advent sermon series. And then every time eschatology is mentioned in a sermon, the preacher can mention "the End with a capital E" or the driving analogy in short order to evoke and reinforce the eschatological "brand."

Or similar to an advertising campaign's goal of enhancing a brand loyalty that already exists, a preacher may think cumulatively about some element of Christian faith, theology, or practice that bears cumulative attention. One of the deepest and most constant concerns of Christians, like all of humanity, is death, the finite limit of all life. The preacher is aware that in the Old Testament there is no overarching view of life after death—simply references to Sheol as the place of the dead—with the human viewed only in bodily terms. In the late Old Testament period there appear to be a few passing references to the idea of resurrection of the body as God's gift of eternal life. This view of the righteous dead being raised at some eschatological future is the dominant view behind and expressed in the New Testament. As the church shifted from its Jewish roots to becoming Gentile and embracing Greco-Roman views, humans were seen more as souls who happened to be caught inside bodies. Postbiblical-era Christians then picked up pieces of biblical language (viewing the world as three-tiered—with heaven above, the world in the middle, and hell below) and connected it with this view of the soul and shaped a theology of saved Christian souls going to heaven when they die and damned souls being sent to hell. In our contemporary, globalized, postmodern culture, Christians pick and choose from Christian and other sources to shape their understanding of God's gift of eternal life in Jesus Christ. Expressions of these theologies can be literal or metaphorical.

Into this complicated historical and contemporary situation, a preacher with sensitivity to postmodern meaning-making might want to affirm the promise of eternal life while giving hearers the freedom to shape their theology for themselves. A cumulative strategy for such an approach might begin with funerals. Regardless of who died or the circumstances of the person's death, the preacher takes the opportunity to correct bad but well-intentioned theology concerning why people die (as if God lovingly wills someone's death so that this person can now be with God) and to affirm the gift of eternal life in broad but strong terms at the same time. The preacher might always refer to Romans 8:31–39 and always say something like,

> In times of grieving, people are likely to offer family and friends words that are meant to be comforting but which distort both the gospel of Jesus Christ and the character of [the person's] life. Words like, "God just needed another angel." Or "God loved _____ so much that God wanted her closer." Or "Well, at least she/he is with God now." These are all wrong. _____ is not with God now. _____ has always been with God, because God has always been with _____. The good news of Jesus Christ is that death has not changed that one iota. When those we care about die, we finite mortals are no longer able to give them our love because we have been separated from them. That's why marriage vows are "'til death do us part." But Paul writes, "Neither death nor life ... nor

> anything else in all creation will be able to separate us from the love of God in Christ Jesus our Lord." That's pretty radical love. God is beyond the limits of mortality. There is nothing we can do and nothing that can happen to us that will make God stop loving us. In the midst of the feelings of confusion, guilt, anger, and sorrow that ache in our bones because _____ died, the good news about God's gift of eternal life that we need to cling to is that God loves her/him as much now in death as God always loved her/him in life.

Funerals, in the midst of grieving, are neither the time to explore different theoretical possibilities concerning eternal life nor to persuade people that a specific view is correct. They are simply times to affirm the good news of God's gift of eternal life in Christ Jesus in broad ways for all to experience grace and comfort.

In sermons distant from the moment of grief, however, preachers might use such an expression as that above as the starting point for deeper reflection: the good news that should inform *any* theology of eternal life is that God loves us in death just as God has loved us in life. This is the repeated umbrella theme of an ongoing brand loyalty campaign, but different sermons might then do very different things underneath that umbrella. In preaching on a biblical text that speaks of the resurrection of the body, the preacher could start by recalling the broad umbrella—explaining the Hebraic view of the human, how the ancient church understood the promise of resurrection, the theology of resurrection still affirmed in the ecumenical creeds, and how it might be understood today. In preaching on a New Testament text that speaks of heaven or hell, a preacher might follow a similar pattern, starting with recalling the broad umbrella theme—explaining the Greco-Roman view of the human, how the postbiblical-era church reinterpreted the promise of resurrection in terms of heaven and hell, the theology of souls with God as dominant theme in historical theology, and how this view might be understood today. In yet another thematic sermon at a different time, the preacher could begin with a reminder of the broad umbrella theme of God's gift of eternal life in loving us beyond the limits of death and then lay out a range of different views of eternal life, including some popular ones in contemporary culture drawn from non-Christian sources. The preacher might name the range of views that fit with Christian faith and theology and which ones do not. Making clear that a range of views is possible (at the very least resurrection and heaven/hell), the preacher might then name her or his view in a way that invites people to consider it without forcing it upon them.

Clearly, thinking and strategizing about both short-term and longer-term approaches can enhance the effectiveness of preaching in significant ways. We should be honest, however, that even cumulative preaching can only be so effective at grounding Christian faith and identity. A twelve- to forty-five-minute sermon each week must compete with noise from the world that is overwhelming. As advertisers have had to find ways to use new and evolving media in spreading their campaigns, so must churches use every means available to spread our message.

Preaching is a unique and powerful tool, but it is not the only form of proclamation the church has at hand. Preachers and church leaders must *coordinate* cumulative themes and issues across proclamatory media. Obvious are communication settings inside the church. How do recurring themes in sermons make their way into Sunday school discussions, youth group retreats, and administrative meeting debates, and vice versa? Less obvious are communication means that speak beyond the walls of the church: newsletters, emails, webpages, and social media. Too often churches primarily focus on these media as tools for marketing the church, its programs, and its special events. But these can all also be loci of evangelism (*euangelion*), teaching (*didache*), and proclamation (*kerygma*). A Facebook post cannot dive into a theme in as detailed a fashion as a sermon any more than a billboard can tell a brand's story in the same way a television commercial can. But the different elements together (sermon plus Facebook post, or commercial plus billboard) are more effective than the sermon or commercial alone. A proclamation campaign can change lives, build the church, and impact the world in ways a singular proclamation event cannot.

Finally, returning to our earlier discussion of the postmodern communication situation in which the world now finds itself, the various media available to the church should not only serve as outlets for proclamation campaigns (as in a linear model of communication) but also as opportunities to listen to the church's "consumers"—members and seekers—as they shape and reshape our cumulative themes and topics and as they initiate new ones that we need to pick up and bring into our sermons (as in a multidirectional model of communication). What discussions about the last sermon series were held in the older adult Sunday school class that might suggest a different sermon series in the future? What political topics that the preacher has been avoiding keep getting discussed among Christian groups on different Facebook threads? What seemingly nontheological interests are expressed in conversation and on social media by the current members of a preacher's empathetic focus group that might invite deeper and recurring theological and existential reflection in the pulpit?

God uses preachers to shape Christian faith, identity, practices, and ethics over the course of sermon upon sermon, Sunday after Sunday, month after month, and year after year. Preachers would do well to listen as God speaks to them through others, suggesting ways of preaching that we might otherwise miss altogether.

Notes

Preface

1. https://pcpe.smu.edu/.

Chapter 1: The Problem

1. Mark Abadi, "11 Dramatic Ways the World Has Changed in the Last 20 Years Alone," *BusinessInsider.com*, March 29, 2018, https:// www.businessinsider.com/progress-innovation-since-1998-2018-3.

2. "Mobile Fact Sheet," *PewResearch.org*, June 12, 2019, https:// www.pewinternet.org/fact-sheet/mobile/.

3. Ryan Holmes, "We Now See 5,000 Ads a Day . . . And It's Getting Worse," *LinkedIn.com*, February 19, 2019, https://www.linkedin .com/pulse/have-we-reached-peak-ad-social-media-ryan-holmes/.

4. See Madan Sarup, *An Introductory Guide to Post-Structuralism and Postmodernism* (Athens: University of Georgia Press, 1993); and Denis McQuail, *Mass Communication Theory: An Introduction* (Newbury Park, CA: Sage Publications, 1994).

5. Roxanne Hovland and Joyce M. Wolburg, *Advertising, Society, and Consumer Culture* (Armonk, NY: M. E. Sharpe, 2010), 69–73.

6. Richard W. Pollay, "The Distorted Mirror: Reflections on the Unintended Consequences of Advertising," *Journal of Marketing* 50, no. 2 (1986): 18–36.

7. "Ad Age Advertising Century: Timeline," *Adage.com*, March 29, 1999, https://adage.com/article/special-report-the-advertising-century /ad-age-advertising-century-timeline/143661.

8. Jef Richards and Catharine Curran, "Oracles on 'Advertising': Searching for a Definition," *Journal of Advertising* 31, no. 2 (2002): 63–77.

9. Sandra Moriarty, Nancy Mitchell, Charles Wood, and William Wells, *Advertising & IMC: Principles and Practices*, 11th ed. (New York: Pearson Education, 2019), 35.

10. Micael Dahlen and Sara Rosengren, "If Advertising Won't Die, What Will It Be? Toward a Working Definition of Advertising," *Journal of Advertising* 45, no. 3 (2016): 334–45.

11. Theodore Levitt, "The Morality of Advertising," *Harvard Business Review*, July–August 1970, 84–92.

12. See https://www.youtube.com/watch?v=hQf578gNueg.

13. For example, TOMS, "For One, Another," September 21, 2015, https://www.youtube.com/watch?v=xkF4X5MfW0w.

14. See www.adcouncil.org.

15. See www.adcouncil.org/Our-Campaigns/The-Classics.

16. See https://www.youtube.com/watch?v=bdQBurXQOeQ.

17. See https://www.youtube.com/watch?v=izZ1ejh1_YI.

Chapter 2: How Communication Has Changed

1. Claude Elwood Shannon, "A Mathematical Theory of Communication," *Bell System Technical Journal* 27.3 (July 1948): 379–423; Claude Elwood Shannon and Warren Weaver, *A Mathematical Theory of Communication* (Champaign: University of Illinois Press), 1949.

2. This description of the linear communication model is adapted from Sandra Moriarty, Nancy Mitchell, Charles Wood, and William Wells, *Advertising and IMC: Principles and Practices*, 11th ed. (New York: Pearson Education), 125.

3. See https://www.youtube.com/watch?v=GcRVDD1Brhc.

4. Broadus's original edition was published by Smith, English & Co. (Philadelphia, 1870). The book was revised by Edwin Charles Dargan with Broadus's approval (New York: A. C. Armstrong, 1898), and again by Jesse Burton Weatherspoon (New York: Harper Brothers, 1944). Vernon Stanfield revised it one final time, but by this point the work had lost much of its influence (New York: Harper One, 1979).

5. Interactive model of communication adapted from Tom Altstiel and Jean Grow, *Advertising Creative: Strategy, Copy, and Design*, 4th ed. (Los Angeles: Sage Publications, 2017), 125.

6. See, for example, Freire, *Pedagogy of the Oppressed*, trans. Myra Bergman Ramos (New York: Herder and Herder, 1970); and hooks, *Teaching to Transgress: Education as the Practice of Freedom* (New York: Routledge, 1994), and *Teaching Community: A Pedagogy of Hope* (New York: Routledge, 2003).

7. See https://www.youtube.com/watch?time_continue=3&v=kNxgxF-7SfA.

8. See William D. Thompson and Gordon C. Bennett, *Dialogue Preaching* (Valley Forge, PA: Judson Press, 1969).

9. Originally published by Abingdon in 1970, the most recent revised and expanded version was published by Chalice Press in 2001.

10. In addition to those scholars discussed here, Ronald J. Allen and O. Wesley Allen, Jr. have identified conversational themes playing a role in the works of numerous homileticians; see *The Sermon without End: A Conversational Approach to Preaching* (Nashville: Abingdon, 2015), 108–14.

11. McClure, *The Roundtable Pulpit: Where Leadership and Preaching Meet* (Nashville: Abingdon, 1995); see also McClure, "Preacher as Host and Guest," in *Slow of Speech and Unclean Lips: Contemporary Images of Preaching Identity*, ed. Robert Stephen Reid (Eugene, OR: Cascade, 2010), 119–43.

12. Rose, *Sharing the Word: Preaching in the Roundtable Church* (Louisville, KY: Westminster John Knox Press, 1997).

13. See R. J. Allen, *Interpreting the Gospel: An Introduction to Preaching* (St. Louis: Chalice, 1998), 65–95, and "Preaching and Mutual Critical Correlation through Conversation," in *Purposes of Preaching*, ed. Jana Childers (St. Louis: Chalice, 2004), 1–22.

14. O. Wesley Allen, Jr., *The Homiletic of All Believers: A Conversational Approach* (Louisville, KY: Westminster John Knox Press, 2005)

Chapter 3: Understanding the Hearer

1. Patty Odell, "Lean Cuisine's Double-Digit Digital Turn-around," *ChiefMarketer.com*, April 6, 2016, https://www.chiefmarketer.com/lean-cuisines-double-digit-digital-turnaround/.

2. Odell, "Lean Cuisine's Double-Digit Digital Turnaround."

3. M. K. de Mooij, *Global Marketing and Advertising: Understanding Cultural Paradoxes*, 4th ed. (Thousand Oaks, CA: Sage, 2019).

4. Hofstede Insights, "Compare Countries," https://www.hofstede-insights.com/product/compare-countries/.

5. Hofstede Insights, "Compare Countries."

6. The information in this table is adapted from http://3age.com.my/wp-content/uploads/2017/02/Multiple-Generations-At-Work-01.jpg. For more on generational differences see Matt Rosenberg, "Gen X, Millennials, and Other Generations through the Years," *ThoughtCo.com*, June 8, 2019, https://www.thoughtco.com/names-of-generations-1435472?print.

7. Hanna Knowles, "The Importance of Generational Targeting: From Millennials to Baby Boomers, One Message Won't Compute," *Medium.com*, November 3, 2017, https://medium.com/madison-ave -collective/the-importance-of-generational-targeting-from-millennials -to-baby-boomers-one-message-wont-69b18c563d3a.

8. See https://youtu.be/eD6yYnZAZcM.

9. Adrianne Pasquarelli, "Real-Time Reaction: Watch Nike's Kae- pernick Ad Expose a Generational Divide," *Adage.com*, September 7, 2018, https://adage.com/article/cmo-strategy/watch-nike-s-kaepernick -ad-expose-a-generational-divide/314874.

10. "Watch Nearly 2,000 Consumers React in Real-Time to Nike's Kaepernick Commercial," *MorningConsult.com*, https://morningconsult .com/form/nike-dial-test/.

11. Bob Curley, "Sugar Cereals Not Just for Breakfast Anymore . . . Millennials Eat Them as a Snack," *Healthline.com*, April 18, 2018, https://www.healthline.com/health-news/sugar-cereals-health-effects#1.

12. de Mooij, *Global Marketing and Advertising*, chapter 3.

13. Strategic Business Insights, "VALS," http://www.strategicbusiness insights.com/vals/ (accessed August 4, 2020).

14. David Sleeth-Keppler, "Use VALS™ to Position a Brand," Strate- gic Business Insights, August 2016, http://www.strategicbusinessinsights .com/vals/free/2016-08brandpositioning.shtml.

15. Lenora Tubbs Tisdale, *Preaching as Local Theology and Folk Art*, Fortress Resources for Preaching (Minneapolis: Fortress, 1997); James R. Nieman, *Knowing the Context*, Elements of Preaching (Minneapolis: Fortress, 2008); for a critique of these types of approaches, see Adam Hearlson, "Are Congregations Texts?" *Homiletic* 39, no. 1 (2014): 19–29.

16. Matthew D. Kim, *Preaching with Cultural Intelligence: Under- standing the People Who Hear Our Sermons* (Grand Rapids: Baker, 2017).

17. James R. Nieman and Thomas E. Rogers, *Preaching to Every Pew: Cross-Cultural Strategies* (Minneapolis: Fortress, 2001).

18. Joseph R. Jeter Jr. and Ronald J. Allen, *One Gospel, Many Ears* (St. Louis: Chalice, 2002).

19. Thomas H. Troeger and H. Edward Everding Jr., *So That All Might Know: Preaching That Engages the Whole Congregation* (Nashville: Abingdon, 2008).

20. Leah D. Schade, *Preaching in the Purple Zone: Ministry in the Red-Blue Divide* (Lanham, MD: Rowman and Littlefield, 2019).

21. For using the Myers-Briggs Type Indicator in preaching, see Robert E. Stiefel, "Preaching to All the People: The Use of Jungian

Typology and the Myers-Briggs Type Indicator," *Anglican Theological Review* 74, no. 2 (1992): 175–202; and Shelley E. Cochran, "The Ear of the Listener," *Homiletic* 18, no. 1 (1993): 7–10.

22. The authors are unaware of any scholarly works applying the Enneagram to preaching, but popular examples are showing up on online, e.g., Ten Thousand Fathers, "Preaching through the Lens of the Enneagram," https://worship.school/blog/preaching-through-the-enneagram.

23. Strategic Business Insights, "The US VALS Survey," http://www.strategicbusinessinsights.com/vals/presurvey.shtml.

24. Arm and Hammer, "Baking Soda: The Small Box with Endless Possibilities," https://www.armandhammer.com/baking-soda?gclid=EAIaIQobChMI8sv5rM7G5AIVWP_jBx2_oABDEAAYASAAEgK1ofD_BwE.

25. "How to Use Laddering in Qualitative Marketing Research," *Focusgrouptips.com,* https://www.focusgrouptips.com/laddering.html.

26. Jonathan Gutman, "A Means-End Chain Model Based on Consumer Categorization Processes," *Journal of Marketing* 46, no. 2 (1982): 60–72.

27. Thomas Grubert, "Laddering: A Technique to Find Out What People Value," *B2BInternational.com*, https://www.b2binternational.com/publications/laddering-technique-find-what-people-value/.

28. E.g., as mentioned earlier, McClure, *The Roundtable Pulpit.*

29. To see one rendering of *The Peaceable Kingdom*, visit https://www.worcesterart.org/collection/American/1934.65.html.

Chapter 4: Advertising and Sermonic Forms

1. The three-point sermon form was discussed earlier as an example of linear communication models.

2. Craddock, *As One without Authority* (Nashville: Abingdon, 1971).

3. Lowry, *The Homiletical Plot: The Sermon as Narrative Art Form* (Atlanta: John Knox, 1980). We return to Lowry below.

4. Mitchell, *Black Preaching* (Philadelphia: Lippincott, 1970).

5. Buttrick, *Homiletic: Moves and Structures* (Philadelphia: Fortress, 1987).

6. Ronald J. Allen, ed., *Patterns of Preaching: A Sermon Sampler* (St. Louis: Chalice, 1998); O. Wesley Allen, Jr., *Determining the Form: Structures for Preaching*, Elements of Preaching (Minneapolis: Fortress, 2008); Alyce M. McKenzie, *Novel Preaching: Tips from Top Writers on*

Crafting Creative Sermons (Louisville, KY: Westminster John Knox Press, 2010).

7. Richard Vaughn, "How Advertising Works: A Planning Model," *Journal of Advertising Research* 20, no. 5 (1980): 27–33.

8. Vaughn, "How Advertising Works," 30.

9. William F. Arens, David H. Schaefer, and Michael F. Weigold, *M: Advertising*, 3rd ed. (New York: McGraw-Hill, 2017), 138–40.

10. Arens, Schaefer, and Weigold, *M*, 138–40.

11. McMickle, *Shaping the Claim: Moving from Text to Sermon*, Elements of Preaching (Minneapolis: Fortress, 2008).

12. See https://www.youtube.com/watch?v=G2s0RPrdB_8&feature =youtu.be (accessed August 4, 2020).

13. David Griner, "How Geico Became the One Advertiser It's OK to Love," *Adweek.com*, February 5, 2019, https://www.adweek.com /agencies/how-geico-became-the-one-advertiser-its-ok-to-love/.

14. Greg Jarboe, "GEICO Hump Day Commercial Dominates Social Video, At Least on Wednesdays," *Searchenginewatch.com*, July 24, 2013, https://www.searchenginewatch.com/2013/07/24/geico-hump -day-commercial-dominates-social-video-at-least-on-wednesdays/.

15. Karen Aho, "Geico's Silly Ads Are Working," *Bloomberg.com*, July 25, 2014, https://www.bloomberg.com/news/articles/2014-07-24 /geico-spent-935-million-on-advertising-in-2013-and-it-worked.

16. For a discussion of the ad, see Max Sutherland and Alice K. Sylvester, *Advertising and the Mind of the Consumer* (Sydney: Allen & Unwin, 2000), 99–100.

17. See Taylor Prewitt, "12 Unforgettable Lessons from Legendary Advertiser, David Ogilvy," *Envision-creative.com*, October 10, 2017, https://www.envision-creative.com/david-ogilvy-advertising-lessons/.

18. See https://www.youtube.com/watch?v=AdwvVbQ3tto&feature =youtu.be.

19. Mind over Media, Analyzing Contemporary Propaganda, https://propaganda.mediaeducationlab.com/rate/1379.

20. See https://www.youtube.com/watch?v=m2KECJv9XrQ.

21. Kenneth Hein, "Coke Tells the World to 'Open Happiness,'" *AdWeek.com*, January 22, 2009, https://www.adweek.com/brand -marketing/coke-tells-world-open-happiness-98112/.

22. Frenay, "Importance of Emotions in Advertising."

23. Frenay, "Importance of Emotions in Advertising."

24. See https://www.youtube.com/watch?v=uGJGQQVNqjg.

25. See https://www.youtube.com/watch?v=6wzULnlHr8w.

26. The two homiletical approaches discussed here are gathered under the heading "Valley Sermons," in O. Wesley Allen, Jr., *Determining the Form*, Elements of Preaching (Minneapolis: Fortress, 2008), 55–63.

27. See William B. McClain, *Come Sunday: The Liturgy of Zion* (Nashville: Abingdon, 1990), 62–70.

28. For a revised version of Lowry's work, see *The Homiletical Plot: The Sermon as Narrative Art Form*, expanded version (Louisville, KY: Westminster John Knox Press, 2000).

29. Preachers with different theological orientations will interpret what it means to speak of God's actions in very different ways, but the distinction between proclamation and exhortation holds across the spectrum.

30. Sheldon W. Sorge, "Are We Having Fun Yet?" *Hungry Hearts* 18, no. 1 (Winter 2009): 5.

Chapter 5: Sermonic Imagery and Narrative Advertising

1. Scott Donaton, "Why Brands Need to Skip the Ads and Start Telling Stories," *Adweek.com*, April 19, 2016, https://www.adweek.com/brand-marketing/why-brands-need-skip-ads-and-start-telling-stories-170905/.

2. See Lisa Cron, *Wired for Story: The Writer's Guide to Using Brain Science to Hook Readers from the Very First Sentence* (Berkeley, CA: Ten Speed Press, 2012); and Jonathan Gottshall, *The Storytelling Animal: How Stories Make Us Human* (Boston: Mariner, 2013).

3. Jennifer Edson Escalas, "Imagine Yourself in the Product: Mental Simulation, Narrative Transportation, and Persuasion," *Journal of Advertising* 33, no. 2 (2004): 37–48.

4. Thomas Vogel, *Breakthrough Thinking* (Cincinnati, OH: Simon and Schuster, 2014).

5. Melanie C. Green and Timothy C. Brock, "The Role of Transportation in the Persuasiveness of Public Narratives," *Journal of Personality and Social Psychology* 79, no. 5 (2000): 701–21.

6. This example is inspired by Ana Gotter, "Storytelling: The Key to Effective Advertising," *Disruptiveadvertising.com*, August 22, 2017, https://www.disruptiveadvertising.com/marketing/storytelling-advertising/.

7. "The Science of Storytelling," *OneSpot.com*, July 1, 2017, https://www.onespot.com/blog/infographic-the-science-of-storytelling/.

8. "The Science of Storytelling."

9. Sarah Walker, "The Power of Storytelling," *MillwardBrown.com*, https://www.millwardbrown.com/docs/default-source/insight-documents

/points-of-view/Millward_Brown_POV_The-Power-of-Storytelling
.pdf.

10. Gotter, "Storytelling."

11. Frenay, "Importance of Emotions in Advertising."

12. Vogel, *Breakthrough Thinking*.

13. Chip Heath and Dan Heath, *Made to Stick: Why Some Ideas Survive and Others Die* (New York: Random House, 2008).

14. Vogel, *Breakthrough Thinking*, 81–84.

15. Vogel, *Breakthrough Thinking*, 81–84.

16. Vogel, *Breakthrough Thinking*, 82.

17. Vogel, *Breakthrough Thinking*, 81–84.

18. After eight years, Subway discontinued using Jared Fogle as their spokesperson in 2017 when he was arrested as a sex offender.

19. "Learn about Narrative Arcs: Definition, Examples, and How to Create a Narrative Arc in Your Writing," MasterClass.com, September 19, 2019, https://www.masterclass.com/articles/what-are-the-elements-of-a-narrative-arc-and-how-do-you-create-one-in-writing.

20. Vogel, *Breakthrough Thinking*, 83.

21. Gotter, "Storytelling."

22. Gotter, "Storytelling."

23. Evelyn Timson, "The 5 Elements of Narrative Structure That Brands Use to Inspire Prospects," *JeffBullas.com*, February 28, 2018, https://www.jeffbullas.com/narrative-structure/.

24. See https://www.youtube.com/watch?v=InK1MTbUJMc.

25. Jessie Gould, "Don't Sell, Entertain: The Effectiveness of Entertaining Ads," *LT.com*, May 24, 2014, https://www.laneterralever.com/blog/dont-sell-entertain-the-effectiveness-of-entertaining-ads#gref.

26. For a brief overview of the New Homiletic, see O. Wesley Allen, Jr., "Introduction: The Pillars of the New Homiletic," in *The Renewed Homiletic*, ed. O. Wesley Allen, Jr. (Minneapolis: Fortress, 2010), 1–18.

27. David L. Bartlett, "Showing Mercy," in *What's the Matter with Preaching Today?* ed. Mike Graves (Louisville, KY: Westminster John Knox Press, 2004), 23–36.

28. Paul Suggett, "Creative Exercises to Get the Wheels Turning," *TheBalanceCareers.com*, October 14, 2019, https://www.thebalancecareers.com/creative-brain-exercises-39352.

29. For examples of microfiction, see Microfiction Monday Magazine, https://microfictionmondaymagazine.com/; for advice on writing

microfiction, see https://medium.com/the-backstages-of-writing/how
-to-write-micro-fiction-6b204cc9bc2e.

30. See https://www.flipitcap.com/.

31. Vogel, *Breakthrough Thinking*.

32. Sandra Moriarty, Nancy Mitchell, Charles Wood, and William Wells, *Advertising & IMC: Principles and Practices*, 11th ed. (New York: Pearson Education, 2019), chapter 9.

33. Vogel, *Breakthrough Thinking*, 57.

34. Vogel, *Breakthrough Thinking*, 58.

35. Moriarty et al., *Advertising & IMC*, chapter 9.

36. See https://www.youtube.com/watch?v=X4GZfvXx9Js.

37. Edward De Bono, *Six Thinking Hats*, rev. ed. (New York: Bay Back Books, 1999); see Vogel, *Breakthrough Thinking*, 55–57, for a discussion of De Bono.

Chapter 6: Advertising Campaigns and Cumulative Preaching

1. "Advertising Campaign: Find Out How to Develop an Advertising Campaign and Which Strategy Best Fits Your Business," *Cyberclick.es*, https://www.cyberclick.es/en/advertising/advertising-campaign.

2. "Effective Advertisement Campaign Planning & Strategy Ideas," *Storygize.com*, https://www.storygize.com/advertisement-campaign/.

3. Tom Altstiel and Jean Grow, *Advertising Creative: Strategy, Copy, and Design*, 4th ed. (Los Angeles: Sage Publications, 2017), 171–72.

4. Altstiel and Grow, *Advertising Creative*, 171–72.

5. Altstiel and Grow, *Advertising Creative*, 171–72.

6. Altstiel and Grow, *Advertising Creative*, 171–72.

7. Altstiel and Grow, *Advertising Creative*, 171–72.

8. Jeremy Mullman, "Travelers Reunites with Red Umbrella," *Adage.com*, February 13, 2007, https://adage.com/article/news/travelers-reunites-red-umbrella/114972.

9. Erik Oster, "Travelers Insurance Tugs on Heartstrings with Emotional 'Stories of Care,'" *Adweek.com*, 2019, https://www.adweek.com/creativity/travelers-insurance-tugs-on-heartstrings-with-emotional-stories-of-care/.

10. See https://www.travelers.com/about-travelers/commercials.

11. "Diamond Shreddies, An Unbelievable Rebranding Case Study," *Fameable.com*, 2008, https://fameable.com/diamond-shreddies-rebranding-case-study/144/.

12. "Old Spice Case Study: How a 75-Year-Old Brand Changed Digital Marketing Forever," *DigitalTrainingAcademy.com*, 2011, http://www.digitaltrainingacademy.com/casestudies/2011/06/old_spice_case_study_how_a_75yearold_brand_changed_digital_marketing_forever.php.

13. "Marketing Campaign Success—Old Spice," *Transformation Marketing Admin*, April 20, 2015, https://www.transformationmarketing.com/marketing-campaing-success-old-spice/.

14. "Old Spice Case Study."

15. "Old Spice Case Study."

16. William F. Arens, David H. Schaefer, and Michael F. Weigold, *M: Advertising*, 3rd ed. (New York: McGraw-Hill, 2017), 348.

17. Arens, Schaefer, and Weingold, 348.

18. Jeffry Pilcher, "Say It Again: Messages Are More Effective When Repeated," *Thefinancialbrand.com*, September 30, 2014, https://thefinancialbrand.com/42323/advertising-marketing-messages-effective-frequency/.

19. Max Sutherland and Alice K. Sylvester, *Advertising and the Mind of the Consumer* (Sydney: Allen & Unwin, 2000), 155–56.

20. "Do TV Ads 'Wear Out'?" *MillwardBrown.com*, 2012, https://www.r-trends.ru/netcat_files/File/MillwardBrown_KnowledgePoint_DoTvAdsWearout.pdf; "Advertising Wear-Out," *Ipsos.com*, 2004, https://www.ipsos.com/en-us/advertising-wear-out.

21. In *Sermon Treks: Trailways to Creative Preaching* (Nashville: Abingdon, 2013), Ronald J. Allen evaluates and proposes strategies related to a variety of ways to organize sermons for cumulative effect, including the lectionary, preaching through a book of the Bible, using the African American lectionary, the chronology of the Bible, sermon series that start with the Bible, doctrinal preaching, and free selection of text or themes.

22. In *Preaching and Reading the Lectionary: A Three-Dimensional Approach to the Liturgical Year* (St. Louis: Chalice, 2007), O. Wesley Allen, Jr. analyzes ways the Revised Common Lectionary invites a cumulative approach to preaching and suggests strategies for preaching in a series fashion for each season of the three-year lectionary cycle; see also *A Preacher's Guide to Lectionary Sermon Series: Thematic Plans for Years A, B, and C*, vols. 1 and 2 (Louisville, KY: Westminster John Knox Press, 2016, 2019).

23. In his essay "Crafting a Sermon Series: Contemporary Approaches to Structuring Preaching over Time," in *Questions Preachers Ask: Essays in Honor of Thomas G. Long*, ed. Scott Black Johnston and Leonora Tubbs

Tisdale (Louisville, KY: Westminster John Knox Press, 2016), Scott Black Johnston reviews various approaches to series, including the hot topic, expository series, topical/expository hybrid, congregational response series, doctrinal series, liturgical series, and historical series.

24. See O. Wesley Allen, Jr., *Preaching and the Human Condition: Loving God, Self, and Others* (Nashville: Abingdon, 2016).

Printed in the USA
CPSIA information can be obtained
at www.ICGtesting.com
LVHW010541281223
767267LV00011B/46